IMAGES
of America

HISTORIC CHURCHES
OF
ASHTABULA COUNTY

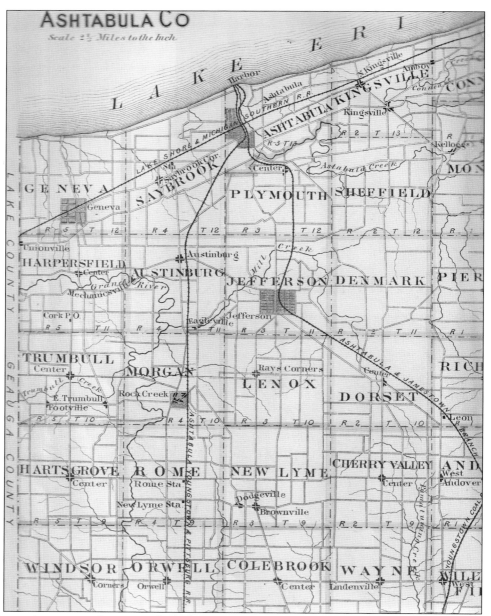

MAP OF ASHTABULA COUNTY. Ashtabula County is the largest county in the state of Ohio. Located at the extreme northeast corner of the state, it is divided into 28 five-mile-square townships (except those that abut Lake Erie), just as laid out by the original surveyors in 1796. (*History of Ashtabula County*, Williams Brothers, 1878.)

ON THE COVER: THE CONGREGATION OF FIRST CONGREGATIONAL CHURCH, 1920S. The first church to be organized in the Ashtabula County seat of Jefferson, Ohio, was the Congregational Church. Early church members included prominent local business and professional men as well as US congressmen and a senator. First Congregational Church was a strident supporter of the abolitionist and suffrage causes. (Courtesy of the Jefferson Historical Society.)

IMAGES
of America

HISTORIC CHURCHES
OF
ASHTABULA COUNTY

Sandy Mitchell Pavick

ARCADIA
PUBLISHING

Published by Arcadia Publishing
Charleston, South Carolina

Printed in the United States of America

Library of Congress Control Number: 2024936639

For all general information, please contact Arcadia Publishing:
Telephone 843-853-2070
Fax 843-853-0044
E-mail sales@arcadiapublishing.com

Visit us on the Internet at www.arcadiapublishing.com

*To the people of Christ Church and St. Peter Church, my
combined church family, who inspire and encourage me*

CONTENTS

ACKNOWLEDGMENTS

Thanks to the many Ashtabula County churches that opened their archives and photo albums to me, as well as to the clergy and lay leaders who took the time to share their church history and tell me stories of their congregations over the years.

Two things became abundantly clear as I spoke with clergy, church leaders, and "rank and file" church members around Ashtabula County. To a person, they are passionate about their churches, and, as I asked about their community outreach programs, all wished that they had the people, energy, and financial resources to do more (although most churches do a lot with the resources available to them.)

I am also struck by the enormous contribution women made in the history of the county's churches, even in eras where women were not given an opportunity to serve in traditional leadership roles.

Particular thanks to the Reverend Peter W. Nielsen III, the Reverend Dr. C. Thomas Jackson, the Reverend Dawson Moorer, Martha Shippy, Ginny Siefert, Annette Sheldon, Venie Hinson, Andrew Holt Frazier, Melanie Todd, pastor Robin Stanley, Norma Waters, Fred Leitert, Kathy Warnes, Carrie Wimer, Rev. John M. Germaine, Barbara Renn, and pastor Aaron Drew as well as the helpful staff and volunteers at the Ashtabula County Historical Society, Harbor-Topky Library, Grand River Public Library, the Jefferson Historical Society, and the Ashtabula County District Library.

Thanks also to my good friend Joanne Humphrey, who came up with the idea for the book and goaded me into writing it.

And, of course, thanks to my husband, Steve, who not only helped proofread but has patiently listened to months of stories about "what I learned today."

The collective church community of Ashtabula County is doing all sorts of things, large and small, to make a positive impact in our little corner of the world. If you have not already, I hope you will consider donating your time, energy, ideas, and/or treasure to a church near you. Together, we can make a difference.

A portion of all book sales will be donated to Ashtabula County food pantries.

INTRODUCTION

Faith was and continues to be a major part of the history of Ashtabula County. This county, in the far northeast corner of the state, is Ohio's largest county and one of the first to be settled by those of European descent.

The earliest European settlers in Ashtabula County came from New England, mostly from Connecticut, in the early 19th century, when the county was part of the Connecticut Western Reserve territory. It is no coincidence that many of the county's place names, such as Andover, New Lyme, and Plymouth, have corresponding places in Connecticut. It should also be no surprise that many of the older churches in this area look like they could have been plucked out of a Connecticut town square. The vast majority of these early settlers were Christian, and the Methodist, Episcopal, and Congregational denominations were well represented.

Later, in the late 19th and early 20th centuries, European immigrants arrived in Ashtabula County, drawn largely by the ample and lucrative jobs available at the Ashtabula Harbor docks, the railroad, and the many area manufacturing plants. The majority of these new residents came from Finland, Denmark, Sweden, and Italy. They too brought their faith. Soon, new Lutheran and Roman Catholic congregations began to appear around the county.

Keeping track of the churches in the county can sometimes be confusing. Several churches have changed denominations over the years. Other denominations have merged or disappeared altogether. For example, many churches in the county still have the Methodist Episcopal denomination etched or carved into their structures. This denomination, which is distinct from the Episcopal Church, merged with the United Brethren Church in 1968 to form today's United Methodist Church (UMC). More recently, several Methodist Churches have split from the UMC and dropped the "United" from their names. The Congregational Church partnered with the Presbyterian Church in forming "frontier" churches in the 19th century. In 1957, the Congregational Church combined with the Evangelical and Reformed (E&R) Church to form the United Church of Christ (UCC). (Note: the E&R Church and the UCC are different from most congregations that call themselves evangelical today.)

There are also differences among Lutheran Churches. Historically, there were several Lutheran governing bodies (called synods) as well as strong national ties, such as German, Danish, Swedish, and Finnish. Today, there are two main governing bodies in the Lutheran Church in the United States—the smaller, more conservative Lutheran Church–Missouri Synod and the Evangelical Lutheran Church in America (ELCA). This partially explains the large number of Lutheran churches in the county.

It is impossible to separate the history of churches from the history of the people of Ashtabula County. The first clergy to preach in Ashtabula County were circuit riders, men who served multiple congregations, many of which were small groups that met in individual church members' homes. These preachers were relatively well-paid but had a hard life. Travel was difficult in Ohio in the early to mid-19th century, and many preachers "lived rough" (slept under the stars) when they were away from their home bases.

It was not just the clergy who faced difficult environments. Most, if not all, of the early churches lacked a heating source. This was at a time when the sermon alone could run 60 to 90 minutes. It was not unusual for worshippers to bring hot coal or hot rocks to church to keep their hands and feet warm during the service. In addition, since it took a sizable amount of money and time to create pews, worshippers stood through the entire service at most of the first churches. When there were pews, they were usually made of rough-hewn logs with no backs to them.

The congregations of the city churches lived a much different life than those who belonged to churches in the more rural areas. Many of the city churches of the mid- to late 19th century had members with money—professional men, large landholders, and wealthy merchants. These congregations hired the best craftsmen and artisans to create their places of worship. In the country churches, it was largely the church members who built the churches, laboring after a long day in the fields to raise the church walls, lay the flooring, and hoist the cast iron bells up to the top of the belfries.

Many of the first Ashtabula County churches had connections to the Underground Railroad, the grassroots system that transported and housed enslaved persons fleeing the American South, roughly 100 miles south of Ashtabula County in (then) Virginia, to freedom in Canada, just across Lake Erie.

There are more than 100 churches in the county that can trace their origin back at least a century. Some are much older. Most of these congregations have met the challenges of the modern age and continue to worship together, reach out to help those in need in their communities, and even thrive.

Sadly, a few historic churches in Ashtabula County have closed their doors. However, most of these churches have left a positive impact on the county. Some former churches have found new lives and purposes as museums, retail establishments, and even theaters. Having this many repurposed churches is somewhat unique to this county. While other counties in Northeast Ohio have one or two repurposed churches, few, if any, have the collection found here in Ashtabula County.

The question of what the first church in the county was is open to some debate. Several congregations claim this designation. Some of the confusion comes from what is considered a church's origination date. Is it the date a few worshippers met in someone's home? Is it the date a minister/pastor/priest first gave a sermon to the congregation? Is it when the congregation organized with a religious group? Or is it when a building was constructed and dedicated? This book shares the claims of all area churches and does not attempt to solve this conundrum.

This book looks at all three categories of Ashtabula County churches. It is important to note that it is the congregation (the group of worshipers) that makes up a church, not the structure. As intriguing as stained-glass windows, hand-hewn pews, and elegant stonework can be, it is the people who continue to be the heart and soul of Ashtabula County's churches.

For the purposes of this book, "historic" is defined as a church that has at least a 100-year-old history. For that reason, many of the primarily African American churches and Evangelical churches are not included. That there are no Jewish or Muslim congregations included is not an oversight. There simply were no such congregations in Ashtabula County a century ago.

There are many more 100-year-old churches in Ashtabula County than the ones profiled here, but these are representative of the people and the structures that shaped the religious communities in extreme Northeast Ohio.

One

Historic Churches Meeting the Challenges of the 20th and 21st Centuries

The first churches in Ashtabula County were of the Congregationalist, Methodist, and Presbyterian denominations, followed closely by the Episcopal, Baptist, and Roman Catholic churches. Many of these are interrelated. For instance, the Congregationalists and the Presbyterians worked closely together in the early Western Reserve, often sharing the same ministers.

The first settlers in the county were in Harpersfield, followed shortly thereafter by Austinburg, Windsor, and Conneaut (originally called Salem). The history of the county's churches mirrors this progression. Villages grew up eventually in Ashtabula, Geneva, and Jefferson, although most of these were small, rather wild population centers carved out of the forests until after the end of the Civil War.

The city of Ashtabula was called the "City of Churches" in the late 19th century. It is easy to see why the city had this moniker. In downtown alone, there were half a dozen elegant churches within a four-block area.

Jefferson, the county seat, was a rugged area when the first churches were organized. The (then) village had fewer than 300 residents in the 1830s when the first groups of worshippers came together.

The more rural areas, such as Kingsville, Hartsgrove, and Orwell, struggled to support multiple denominations until that practice became less and less feasible economically. In most cases, worshippers combined their efforts into a single nondenominational congregation.

Today, the churches that have met the challenges of the 20th and now 21st centuries are finding new and time-honored ways to meet the needs of the communities they serve. Some have food pantries and clothing banks; others offer free community dinners and vacation Bible schools for kids in the summer. Virtually all Ashtabula County churches work diligently to help make life a little easier for those in their communities.

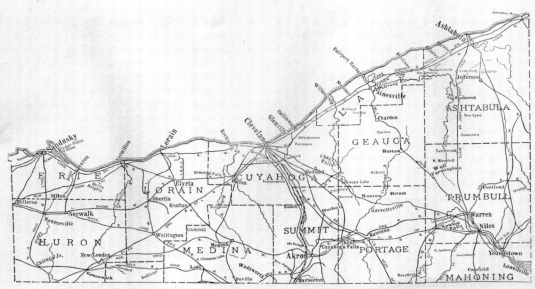

MAP OF WESTERN RESERVE WITH PRESENT COUNTIES PROJECTED ON IT

MAP OF THE WESTERN RESERVE. It is impossible to talk about historic churches, or any early history of Ashtabula County, Ohio, without first talking about the Western Reserve. This section of land, originally part of the Ohio Territory, had been granted to the then Colony of Connecticut by King Charles II as part of the Connecticut Colony's charter. This land became known as the Connecticut Western Reserve, New Connecticut, or simply, the Western Reserve. This piece of land stretched from the Pennsylvania-Ohio state line 120 miles west to Sandusky Bay and south to the 41st parallel. It included today's Ashtabula, Trumbull, Geauga, Cuyahoga, Lake, Lorain, Huron, and Erie Counties. After the Revolutionary War, most of this 3,366,921-acre parcel of land was purchased by a group of private investors known as the Connecticut Land Company for $1.2 million. (*History of Ohio*, Charles B. Galbreath, 1929.)

GEN. MOSES CLEAVELAND. The Connecticut Land Company was one of several corporations formed to survey, divide, and sell the new land out west that was viewed as free for the taking. The Connecticut Land Company sent surveyor Gen. Moses Cleaveland, an investor himself, with a group of 11 to map the Western Reserve and divide the land into five-mile-square parcels. Cleaveland would first set foot in the territory in 1796 when he and his party landed at the mouth of the Conneaut River, in the extreme northeast corner of what is now Ashtabula County. (Cleaveland would later travel to the Cuyahoga River and lend his name—without the "a"—to the village that became Cleveland, Ohio, roughly 120 miles to the east of Conneaut.) (*Sketches of Western Reserve Life*, Harvey Rice, 1885.)

COL. ALEXANDER HARPER. Northeast Ohio in the early 19th century was a wilderness, with dense, dark forests, deep ravines, and creeks that rushed with water in the spring. In 1797, Col. Alexander Harper formed the first permanent settlement in what is now Harpersfield Township. He died in 1798 of malaria and was buried in a hollowed-out log in Unionville. The cemetery on State Route 84 now bears his name. (Author's collection.)

WESTERN RESERVE LOG CABIN. Early settlers in the Western Reserve constructed one-room log cabins like the one pictured above for their family dwellings until more permanent homes could be constructed. Many of the first church meetings and worship services were held in cabins like this. This replica was part of the Austinburg Country Days parade. (Courtesy of Austinburg First United Church of Christ.)

The Rev. Joseph Badger

REV. JOSEPH BADGER. One of the most fascinating characters in early Western Reserve history is Joseph Badger. Badger was a veteran of the American Revolutionary War, where he served at Bunker Hill and with Gen. George Washington when he crossed the Delaware River. After the war, Badger studied theology at Yale University and was the pastor at a Connecticut church for more than a decade. In 1800, he was appointed by the Connecticut Missionary Society to tour the Western Reserve and assess the potential for church growth there. The man must have been indefatigable, especially given the state of travel in Ashtabula County in the early 19th century. More than a dozen area churches count Reverend Badger as their founding father, including Austinburg First United Church of Christ, First Presbyterian Church of Ashtabula, the Congregational Church in Conneaut, and Kingsville Presbyterian Church. (Courtesy of Austinburg First United Church of Christ.)

REV. JOSEPH BADGER RIDING THE CIRCUIT. Reverend Badger began the 600-mile journey on horseback from Connecticut to the Western Reserve on November 15, 1800. His diary indicates he encountered snow so deep that he periodically had to dismount and break the drifts so his horse could continue. When Badger arrived, he found two families in Austinburg, two in Harpersfield Township, and three in Windsor. He traveled as far as the Huron River and concluded his first journey in August 1801, writing, "I have now visited and preached the Gospel to all families in the Western Reserve." Badger returned in 1801 with his wife, Lois, and six children and set about organizing congregations. He was paid $7 a week by the Connecticut Missionary Society plus a plot of land near Austinburg. His first project was to establish a Congregational Church in Austinburg. (Courtesy of Austinburg First United Church of Christ.)

FIRST UNITED CHURCH OF CHRIST. The First United Church of Christ in Austinburg began as a Congregational Church. Founded in 1801 with 16 members, it is the oldest church in the Western Reserve and the second oldest Congregational Church in Ohio. The church's first services were held in two log cabins located near US Route 45 and Lampson Road until a permanent church structure could be built. The pulpit of the original church was elevated and accessed by a spiral staircase. The church also had boxlike pews that were raised above the aisles. (Both, courtesy of Austinburg First United Church of Christ.)

JOSEPH BADGER

Rev. Joseph Badger in "Retirement." For eight years, Reverend Badger traveled the circuit preaching at services and performing pastoral duties all over the Western Reserve. His name appears over and over in the history of early churches in Ashtabula County. Badger left the circuit in 1809 to devote his time to missionary work among the Wyandots and other indigenous people of the area. According to his diary, his work among the Wyandots led 800 members of the tribe to refrain from organizing with Chief Tecumseh when the chief urged tribespeople not to negotiate with European settlers. Badger later served as a chaplain during the War of 1812, at Gen. William Henry Harrison's request. Badger would "retire" in 1810 to Ashtabula Village, where he was instrumental in founding a Presbyterian church there and in Kingsville. Near the end of his life, he retired again, this time to be near his daughter in Wood County, Ohio. Badger died in 1846 at the age of 89. He is buried at Fort Meigs Cemetery in Perrysburg, Ohio. (Courtesy of Austinburg First United Church of Christ.)

SYCAMORE HILL, HOME OF ELIPHALET AND SIBBEL AUSTIN. Facing the need for a new preacher after Badger left Austinburg in 1809, Sibbel Austin, the wife of Austinburg founder Eliphalet Austin, traveled back to the Austins' former hometown of Bristol, Connecticut, on horseback riding side saddle, to find a replacement. This was not an easy journey, and she brought along her newborn daughter, who was still nursing. She appealed to Sally Cowles, the wife of Rev. Giles H. Cowles, to attempt to entice the family to come west to Ohio. (Of course, it would have been unseemly in that era for Sibbel to meet directly with Reverend Cowles.) The Cowles family decided to make the move west and arrived in 1811. The house built by Sibbell and Eliphalet Austin, Sycamore Hill (pictured above), still stands along US Route 45 near State Route 307 in Austinburg. The house has a large room off the porch that was used to hide escaping slaves during the mid-19th century. (Author's collection.)

Edwin W Cowles

REV. GILES HOOKER COWLES. Rev. Giles Cowles was educated at Yale and graduated in 1789. He began preaching in Bristol, Connecticut, in 1791. Cowles married shortly thereafter and proceeded to have eight children in 16 years. Faced with a large family to support, Cowles accepted the offer from the Congregational Church in Austinburg, as it was willing to pay $200 a year for a preacher with an additional $200 being kicked in by the Connecticut Missionary Society. That was more than three times what Cowles was making in Bristol. The offer also included 80 acres of land for a parsonage. The church was permitted to pay the pastor at least partly in produce rather than in cash. At the time they made the move to Ohio in 1811, the Cowles family included Cowles's wife, Sally, Edwin (17, pictured above as an adult), Sally (15), William (13), Edward (10), Martha (7), twins Cornelia and Lysander (4), and Betsy (1). A ninth child, Lewis, was born in Austinburg in 1812. (Courtesy of Austinburg First United Church of Christ.)

THE COWLES HOME. Church members quickly built a log cabin for the Cowles family when they arrived in Austinburg. In 1815, the family replaced those rough accommodations with a large Western Reserve–style farmhouse. That house is standing today and is owned by descendants of Reverend Cowles. It sits near the southwest corner of US Route 45 and Lampson Roads in Austinburg. (*History of Ashtabula County*, Williams Brothers, 1878.)

BETSY MIX COWLES. Betsy Mix Cowles, the youngest daughter of Rev. Giles Cowles, was a prominent suffragist, abolitionist, and teacher. She died in 1876 at age 66, shortly after the present Austinburg Church was finished. Her funeral was the first service held in that church. The Cowles children all stayed in the Western Reserve. Edwin became a pastor. A grandson, also named Edwin, founded the *Cleveland Leader* newspaper. (*History of Ashtabula County*, Williams Brothers, 1878.)

BETSY COWLES'S PARLOR. There is an interesting side note to the Betsy Cowles story. She never married and lived her entire life in the family home. When she died, she requested that her parlor be left as it was. Her descendants have honored those wishes. The parlor still has the original wallpaper, floor coverings, and furniture, including a set of original Hitchcock chairs and a Lincoln rocker. (Author's collection.)

REVEREND COWLES. In addition to being the longtime pastor at the Austinburg church, Rev. Giles Cowles was instrumental in founding eight other Ashtabula County Congregational and Presbyterian Churches: Conneaut (1819), Rome (1819), Windsor (1824), Colebrook/Orwell (1831), Lenox (1832), Millsford (1832), Andover (1832), and Wayne (1832, pictured here). (Courtesy of the Grand River Public Library Archival Collection.)

First Congregational Church
Wayne, Ashtabula County, Ohio

Founded- October 2, 1832
Centenary Celebrated- October 2, 1932

OLD CONGREGATIONAL CHURCH, AUSTINBURG. The first meetinghouse for the Austinburg congregation was completed in 1824, its construction having been delayed by the War of 1812. The church was modeled after the Norfolk Meeting House in Litchfield, Connecticut, and featured a graceful 96-foot spire. (*History of Ashtabula County*, Williams Brothers, 1878.)

FIRST UNITED CHURCH OF CHRIST, AUSTINBURG. As the population of Ashtabula County moved north in the mid-19th century, the Austinburg congregation shifted their worship services from the old church to a frame building in Austinburg Village that now serves as the Austinburg Town Hall. (Courtesy of Austinburg First United Church of Christ.)

GRAND RIVER INSTITUTE. The history of Grand River Institute (now Academy), which still thrives today, is closely linked to that of the Congregational Church in Austinburg. Rev. Giles Cowles was instrumental in helping to form the school in 1831, and Betsy Cowles taught there. The private secondary school was first situated on the banks of the Grand River in Mechanicsville. In 1835, the school trustees voted to relocate the school since the Mechanicsville site was prone to flooding. The original, two-story school building (pictured below) was moved more than three miles to its present location on State Route 307 by a 100-yoke team of oxen. That building was used until 1973, when it was razed. (Above, courtesy of the Ashtabula County District Library; below, *Historical Sketch*, Grand River Institute, 1924.)

GYMNASIUM
The Original Institute Building.

EAGLEVILLE CHURCH. Differences in doctrine caused the Congregational Church community to splinter and form a second congregation in the early 19th century. This group, called the Independent Congregation Church of Austinburg, met for a time at the Grand River Institute before building their own church on Eagleville Road. That structure (pictured here) still stands and is used by an independent Baptist congregation. (Courtesy of Austinburg First United Church of Christ.)

(1876) CONGREGATIONAL CHURCH AND ANNEX (1932) AUSTINBURG, OHIO

AUSTINBURG FIRST UNITED CHURCH OF CHRIST CHURCH ANNEX. The original church bell, cast in 1888 at the Meneely Bell Foundry in Troy, New York, now sits on the lawn in front of the church. The Felgemaker organ was purchased from the Conneaut Congregational Church in 1900 and transported via bobsled. The church was placed in the National Register of Historic Places in 1979. (Courtesy of Austinburg First United Church of Christ.)

FIRST UNITED CHURCH OF CHRIST SPIRE. The church's two-story Fellowship Hall was added in 1932, complete with Sunday school rooms, a kitchen, and restrooms. The sanctuary was raised, and a full basement was excavated in 1982. (Courtesy of Austinburg First United Church of Christ.)

FIRST UNITED CHURCH OF CHRIST, AUSTINBURG, TODAY. First UCC Church in Austinburg continues to serve the community. The church is well-known for its annual rummage sale as well as its free, monthly community dinners. The church also supports the Geneva Food Pantry, hosts a bake sale during Austinburg Country Days, and stocks blessing boxes and a free little library behind the church. (Courtesy of Austinburg First United Church of Christ.)

GENEVA UNITED METHODIST CHURCH.
Geneva United Methodist Church
traces its roots back to 1816, when
the first itinerant Methodist minister,
Samuel Brown, preached in Ashtabula
County. The first church structure was
erected on the corner of Park Street
and South Broadway Avenue in 1833.
The current church, located across the
street, was dedicated in 1867 with a
14-foot spire. The stained-glass windows
depict stories from the New Testament.
(Author's collection.)

GENEVA UNITED METHODIST CHURCH,
TODAY. The Methodist church continues
to play a vital role in the Geneva
community. The church is well-known
for its Swiss steak dinners during Grape
Jamboree and as the site of the periodic
Kiwanis pancake dinners. The church
hosts the annual Geneva Farmers Market
in front of and behind the church
from mid-May through mid-September.
(Author's collection.)

8800 Congregational Church, Geneva, Ohio

CONGREGATIONAL CHURCH, GENEVA.
The Congregational Church in Geneva (pictured) was established in 1866 on South Eagle Street. In 1949, the church merged with Geneva Baptist Church on South Broadway Avenue to form the United Church in Geneva, a church that is still thriving today. The original Congregational Church building was owned by the Masonic Lodge for many years and is now being transformed into a theater (see page 114). (Author's collection.)

FIRST BAPTIST CHURCH, GENEVA.
First Baptist Church was organized in 1816 with 19 original members and built a church on South Broadway Avenue. The congregation merged with that of the Congregational Church on South Eagle Street on May 12, 1949. The new church became the United Church and was organized under the Church of Christ conventions. The combined church continues to prosper. (Courtesy of the Ashtabula County Historical Society.)

UNITED CHURCH CHOIR, 1978. The United Church is home to an impressive, two-stop chord organ, the focal point of the church's sanctuary. The organ used today is made up of two original organs, the parts of which were combined in the 1960s. The church's organist, Connie Brenneman, has been playing since 1975. (Courtesy of the Pruden family.)

UNITED CHURCH OF GENEVA, TODAY. The United Church of Geneva is well-known in the community for its clothing bank and its Kinder Prep preschool academy. The United Church also hosts a weekly Wednesday night Bible study class. Other church outreach programs include support for the Geneva Food Pantry. (Author's collection.)

CHRISTIAN CHURCH, PARK ST., GENEVA, OHIO.
Published by Ladies' Aid Society, Geneva, Ohio.

PARK STREET CHRISTIAN CHURCH, GENEVA.
Park Street Christian Church is another venerable Geneva house of worship. Established in 1867, it is one of the oldest congregations in the city. The original church building was purchased from the Methodist Church and rolled on logs to its present location in the center of the block. The stained-glass windows and ornate tin ceiling in the sanctuary are original to the building. (Author's collection.)

ASA TURNEY, 1867. Asa Turney was the first lay preacher of the Society of Disciples Church, the original name of Park Street Christian Church. He helped fund the purchase of the church building. The first minister was a young Iowan named James W. Inram. Under his and Turney's leadership, the church grew from the original 35 members to 175 members in less than 10 years. (Courtesy of Park Street Christian Church.)

PROGRESSIVE CLUB, PARK STREET CHRISTIAN CHURCH, 1911. In 1894, the church's name was formally changed to Park Street Church of Christ, and the church had approximately 200 members. The name was again changed in 1951, this time to Park Street Christian Church. (Courtesy of Park Street Christian Church.)

PARK STREET CHRISTIAN CHURCH CHOIR, MID-1950S. By the mid-1950s, Park Street Christian Church had a membership of around 250 and an average Sunday attendance of around 100. That number doubled on Easter Sundays, according to church records. The choir in the 1950s and 1960s was under the direction of the organist, Mrs. William Allen. (Courtesy of Park Street Christian Church.)

LADIES AID SOCIETY, 1960s. Park Street Christian Church was extensively remodeled in 1960. The congregation constructed additions to the rear and east sides of the original church structure, and a vestibule was built onto the southeast corner of the church, changing its entrance way so that worshippers entered from the east. The Ladies Aid Society was instrumental in raising the funds needed for these improvements. (Courtesy of Park Street Christian Church.)

PARK STREET CHRISTIAN CHURCH DURING GRAPE JAMBOREE. Park Street Christian Church is well-known for its homemade lunch items and pies for sale during the citywide Geneva Grape Jamboree celebration. The basement of the church turns into a restaurant on Saturday of the festival, with church members selling things like cabbage and noodles, potato soup, and of course, grape pies. (Courtesy of Park Street Christian Church.)

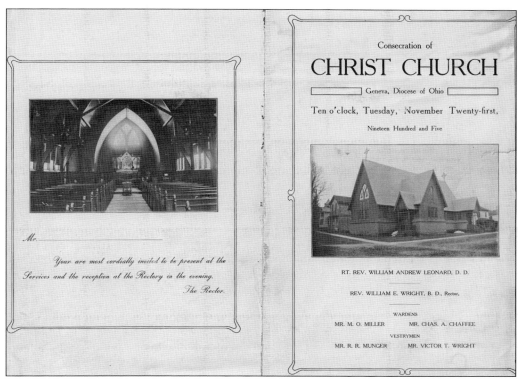

Consecration of

CHRIST CHURCH

Geneva, Diocese of Ohio

Ten o'clock, Tuesday, November Twenty-first,

Nineteen Hundred and Five

RT. REV. WILLIAM ANDREW LEONARD, D. D.

REV. WILLIAM E. WRIGHT, B. D., Rector.

WARDENS

MR. M. O. MILLER   MR. CHAS. A. CHAFFEE

VESTRYMEN

MR. R. R. MUNGER   MR. VICTOR T. WRIGHT

Mr.

Your are most cordially invited to be present at the Services and the reception at the Rectory in the evening.

The Rector.

CHRIST EPISCOPAL CHURCH, GENEVA, DEDICATION SERVICE. Christ Episcopal Church's current structure was built in 1892 at the corner of West Main and South Eagle Streets. A nearby bakery caught fire in 1901 and ignited the church, claiming several of the original leaded-glass windows. The flames were extinguished, and the church structure survived, although char marks are still visible in the basement. (Courtesy of Christ Episcopal Church.)

CHRIST EPISCOPAL CHURCH. In 1941, the church building was rolled up the hill, approximately one-quarter mile, to its present (and much drier) South Eagle Street location. The building was turned 90 degrees, changing the entrance to the left of the church from the street side. (Courtesy of Christ Episcopal Church.)

PARQUET FLOOR AT CHRIST EPISCOPAL CHURCH, GENEVA. The wooden parquet flooring at Christ Episcopal Church comes from Longwood, the Severance family mansion in Cleveland Heights, Ohio, just east of Cleveland. The floorboards were salvaged from the elegant structure before it was razed in 1960 to make way for Severance Center shopping mall. Church members labored for days, salvaging, installing, and refinishing the new floorboards. (Author's collection.)

LONGWOOD MANSION. Longwood, the Severance family home, was built in the 1880s and extensively remodeled in 1917. The Cleveland Heights mansion had more than 50 rooms, including a large library, a drawing room, and a great hall, complete with a pipe organ. The home sat on 125 acres and was well-known for its manicured, European-style gardens. (Courtesy of Cleveland State University/Special Collections.)

CHRIST EPISCOPAL CHURCH INTERIOR. Dubbed the "Little Church with the Big Heart," Christ Episcopal Church has a beautiful, wooden interior. Each pew is adorned by a carved fleur-de-lis, a traditional symbol of the Trinity. The hand-carved lower altar (pictured) comes from the closed St. Michael's Episcopal Church in Unionville. The triptych altar paintings were completed by parishioner Daniel L. Smith in 2012. (Author's collection.)

CHRIST EPISCOPAL CHURCH CHOIR, GENEVA, 1958. Music has always been an integral part of worship services at Christ Episcopal Church. The church is equipped with a chord organ that dates back to 1926. The organ was restored in 1966 and continues to be used for worship services. (Courtesy of Christ Episcopal Church.)

SUNDAY SCHOOL, CHRIST EPISCOPAL CHURCH, 1965. Christian education, both for children and adults, has been a tradition at Christ Episcopal Church since its inception. At one time, the church had multiple Sunday school classes, a vibrant vacation Bible school program, and even a traveling theater program. Today, the church hosts an intergenerational family program called "Faith, Family, Fun" on the second Sunday of each month. (Courtesy of Christ Episcopal Church.)

CHRIST EPISCOPAL CHURCH, TODAY. The congregation at Christ Episcopal Church strives to live up to its "Little Church with the Big Heart" nickname. Church outreach programs include helping area food pantries, cooking and serving with area hunger programs, providing blessing bags, creating prayer shawls and other knitted and crocheted items with the Prayer Shawl Ministry, and helping teen moms. Christ Episcopal Church is also known for its annual Holiday Ticket Auction. (Author's collection.)

UNIONVILLE UNITED CHURCH. Unionville United Church, located just east of County Line Road on State Route 84, is another church that can trace its history back to the work of Joseph Badger. His first sermon in Unionville was given in the home of Unionville founder, Col. Alexander Harper, the first permanent resident of Ashtabula County, in 1800, during Badger's debut trip to the Western Reserve. (Courtesy of Unionville United Church.)

REV. MARY CANDY. An interesting story about Unionville United Church is that the church had one of the first female pastors in the area. Rev. Mary Candy led the congregation in the early 1930s, several decades before most other Christian denominations began ordaining women. Reverend Candy was the widow of Rev. J.F. Candy, a longtime pastor at Geneva Congregational Church. (Courtesy of Unionville United Church.)

UNIONVILLE UNITED CHURCH. The first Unionville United Church structure was built inside Alexander Harper Cemetery in 1830. The present Greek Revival–style church, constructed in 1834, is the oldest church building in continuous use in the Western Reserve. The church originally featured raised pews with doors to enter from the aisles. It also had two box pews on either side of the pulpit, one of which was reserved for the Harper family. In 1846, Rev. Martin Wilcox, upset that church members were arriving late to worship service, commissioned a bell to call people to church. The 900-pound bell, cast in Troy, New York, was hauled to the church from the Port of Fairport Harbor by a team of oxen. The bell is still used on Sundays. (Left, courtesy of Unionville United Church; below, courtesy of J. Humphrey.)

St. John's Lutheran Church, Geneva. The congregation of St. John's Lutheran Church was organized in 1898 and met in parishioner August Pohl's home on State Route 84 until a suitable meetinghouse could be found. The first pastor visited on alternate Sundays, arriving by train. These early worship services were conducted in German, and German services continued to be held into the 1950s. (Courtesy of St. John's Lutheran Church.)

St. John's Lutheran Church. In 1904, the growing group of worshippers began meeting at the Army Hall on East Main Street and North Broadway Avenue in Geneva. Five years later, the congregation shared worship space with Christ Episcopal Church, when that church was still located at the corner of West Main and South Eagle Streets (see page 31). (Courtesy of St. John's Lutheran Church.)

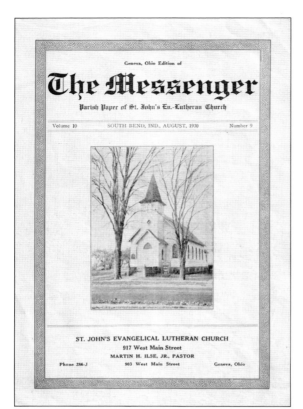

St. John's Lutheran Church Exterior, 1930. On May 13, 1917, the congregation dedicated a church of its own on West Main Street (in the space currently used by Formality Bridal, see pages 122–123). At this point, the congregation numbered 65 members. The church featured a long stall at the rear of the main building to shelter horses and buggies. (Courtesy of St. John's Lutheran Church.)

St. John's Lutheran Church/Geneva Baptist Church. The traditional, wood-frame church featured leaded-glass windows, hand-carved woodwork, and a simple altar framed by a Gothic arch. The Southern Baptist Church in Geneva purchased the property as soon as it was put up for sale in 1962, and the two congregations shared the space for two years. (Courtesy of the Ashtabula County District Library.)

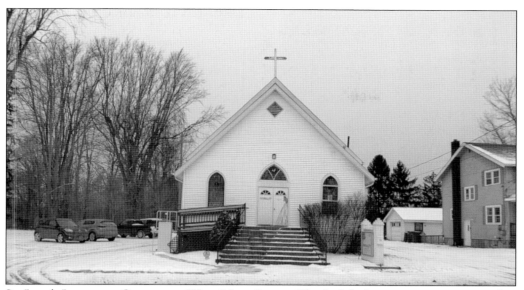

ST. JOHN'S LUTHERAN CHURCH ON WEST MAIN STREET. The St. John's congregation continued to use the church on West Main Street until the current church on South Broadway Avenue was completed in 1964. The church on West Main Street was decommissioned and sold in 2021. What was left of the Baptist congregation combined with the congregation in Eagleville. (Courtesy of St. John's Lutheran Church.)

ALTAR AT ST. JOHN'S LUTHERAN CHURCH, 1964. The 1964 St. John's Lutheran Church features stone from the bed of the Grand River in the interior and exterior of the church. Another prominent feature of the new church was the three-bank Wicks pipe organ, which is still used today. (Courtesy of St. John's Lutheran Church.)

ST. JOHN'S LUTHERAN CHURCH QUILT GUILD. The Quilt Guild at St. John's Lutheran Church is a dynamic ministry that helps to raise money for outreach programs by crafting detailed, unique, decorative quilts that they auction on eBay and other sites. In 2001, guild members created 60 quilts (some of which are pictured here) to raise money for the Lutheran World Relief Fund. (Courtesy of St. John's Lutheran Church.)

ST. JOHN'S LUTHERAN CHURCH, GENEVA, TODAY. St. John's Lutheran Church continues to be a positive influence in the community. The church is home to an active preschool. It also hosts a seasonal produce giveaway program, supports the Geneva Food Pantry, and has a senior outreach program. (Courtesy of Andrew Holt Frazier.)

ASSUMPTION OF THE BLESSED VIRGIN MARY CATHOLIC CHURCH. The few Roman Catholic families in Geneva were originally served by St. Mary's Parish in Painesville. However, the 15-mile trek to church was difficult for parishioners. Eventually, the diocese allowed for mass to be celebrated in private homes. As the number of Catholics in Geneva grew, they began meeting in downtown Geneva, in the Jenny Munger block. (*Our Parish*, Assumption Church, 1965.)

ASSUMPTION OF THE BLESSED VIRGIN MARY CHURCH, TODAY. The current church structure was dedicated in 1927. The modified Doric design of that original design is still visible in the columns beside the church's entrance. The church was extensively modernized in 1965 when light oak pews and air-conditioning were added. (Author's collection.)

SAYBROOK METHODIST CHURCH. The group of worshippers that would become Saybrook Methodist Church was organized in 1816 with around 11 members. They first met in private homes, most often in a barn belonging to the Munson family, and were served by the circuit riders who visited the congregation once every three to four months. The first church building was constructed on the north side of US Route 20, just east of Depot Road in Ashtabula County. The congregation built the present church in 1849 at a cost of $2,000. Originally, the sanctuary had a balcony on the west end and a platform on the east end, but those parts of the structure were removed in 1880 when a choir loft was added. The congregation of Saybrook Methodist Church continues to serve the community. Church outreach programs include summer worship services at Saybrook Park, monthly free community dinners, a Halloween trunk or treat event, and a summer vacation Bible school. (Courtesy of the Ashtabula County District Library.)

ST. PETER EPISCOPAL CHURCH. One of the oldest congregations in Ashtabula County, St. Peter Episcopal Church was formed in 1816 by members of a Plymouth, Connecticut, church of the same name. Services were first held in the log cabin home of John G. Blakeslee (pictured below), which still stands. The first church structure was completed in 1850 on the west side of South Park in Ashtabula. (Courtesy of St. Peter Episcopal Church.)

BLAKESLEE LOG CABIN. Blakeslee Cabin, the home of Sala and John Blakeslee, is the oldest log structure still standing in Ashtabula County. The cabin, built in 1810, is now owned by the Ashtabula Historical Society. The property welcomes the public each September during Log Cabin Days. St. Peter Episcopal Church holds a historically accurate worship service on Sunday morning during this celebration. (Courtesy of the Ashtabula County Historical Society.)

INTERIOR OF THE OLD CHURCH. The first permanent priest at St. Peter Episcopal Church was Rev. Roger Searle, who arrived on February 16, 1817. According to church records, Searle was originally paid in firewood rather than in cash. He remained with the St. Peter congregation until 1824. (Courtesy of the Ashtabula County Historical Society.)

ST. PETER EPISCOPAL CHURCH INTERIOR, 1960s. The current church, designed by the Cleveland architectural firm of Copper, Wade, and Copper, was dedicated in 1965 and built on the same footprint as the original church. It features a 54-seat chapel off the nave and a 1,441-pipe Holtkamp organ, donated by the Carlisle family. The original altar was reinstalled in the new church. (Courtesy of the Ashtabula County District Library.)

St. Peter Episcopal Church Stained-Glass Window. As many stained-glass windows as possible were saved from the old church and reinstalled in the new church structure, including the window dedicated to longtime rector (and Joseph Badger's son-in-law) the Reverend John Hall. To keep their historic integrity, glass for the new stained-glass windows at St. Peter Episcopal Church was handmade by artisans from Germany. (Courtesy of the Ashtabula County Historical Society.)

HOPE AND A FUTURE FOOD PANTRY. Cooking is an integral part of St. Peter Episcopal Church's community outreach. Each Tuesday since 2014, the crew cooks, packages, and distributes up to 150 meals plus grocery items to needy neighbors. The Reverend Peter W. Nielsen III and church volunteers have also created a supportive community among the food pantry patrons. Pictured are, from left to right, Andrew Holt Frazier, Wayne Pelton, Nick Wayman, and Nielsen. (Author's collection.)

ST. PETER EPISCOPAL CHURCH, TODAY. St. Peter Episcopal Church continues to thrive and worship together each Sunday. In addition to Hope and a Future Food Pantry, the church's outreach program, efforts include distributing 250 baskets with dinner preparations each Christmas, offering scholarships for area youth and adults, supporting numerous local charities, providing space for the local Salvation Army offices, and hosting regular free community concerts. (Author's collection.)

FIRST BAPTIST CHURCH, ASHTABULA, 1950s.
The congregation of First Baptist Church in Ashtabula was founded on January 5, 1825, by 39 parishioners from First Baptist Church in Kingsville. The first structure was a frame church at the southwest corner of (now) North Park. A new church was built in 1859 but was destroyed by fire in 1898. The current church was dedicated in 1900. (Courtesy of the Ashtabula County District Library.)

FIRST BAPTIST CHURCH, ASHTABULA. Some of the stained-glass windows at First Baptist Church were created by Tiffany Studios of New York City. The church is well-known for its pipe organ, which was installed in 1915 and is still used today. Nicknamed "the Light on the Corner," the church's outreach programs include a weekday breakfast program for the hungry, camp scholarships for kids, and the Sew Simple quilt ministry. (Courtesy of the Harbor-Topky Library Archives.)

Interior of Capernaum Lutheran as it looked in 1921

CAPERNAUM LUTHERAN CHURCH, ASHTABULA. Messiah Lutheran Church, originally called Evangelical Messiah Lutheran Church of Ashtabula, Ohio, was an offshoot of Capernaum Lutheran Church in Ashtabula Harbor, now Faith Lutheran Church (pictured above). The original 190 members of the church and 130 children, organized on February 18, 1921, were mostly of Swedish descent. (Courtesy of Messiah Lutheran Church.)

HIAWATHA STREET CHAPEL IN 1921

HIAWATHA CHURCH OF GOD IN CHRIST. The first church building for the Messiah Lutheran Church congregation was the Hiawatha Chapel (pictured at left), built in 1903 and located on the corner of Hiawatha Street and Fassett Avenue. The Hiawatha Chapel still stands and is used by the Hiawatha Church of God in Christ congregation. (Courtesy of Messiah Lutheran Church.)

MESSIAH LUTHERAN CHURCH, ASHTABULA. The Hiawatha Chapel continued to be under the Capernaum Lutheran Church until a permanent structure was built for the new congregation that would become Messiah Lutheran. By the end of 1921, the Messiah congregation numbered 326 adults and 141 children. (Courtesy of Messiah Lutheran Church.)

MESSIAH LUTHERAN CHURCH. The current Messiah Lutheran Church building was constructed in 1930. Church leaders voted to build this new structure in mid-1929 right before the October 1929 stock market crash. Suddenly, building funds were much harder to come by, so several church members took out second mortgages on their residences to help fund the construction of the new church. (Courtesy of Messiah Lutheran Church.)

INTERIOR OF MESSIAH LUTHERAN CHURCH. The Messiah Lutheran Church building has vaulted wood truss beams stenciled with traditional Swedish designs, oak floors, a Gothic arch above the altar, and intricate stained-glass windows. A highlight of the Advent season in the 1950s and 1960s was the huge, decorated evergreen tree installed in the sanctuary. (Courtesy of Messiah Lutheran Church.)

THE REVEREND HOWARD W. PETTERSON. The Reverend Petterson (pronounced pet-er-son) was one of Messiah Lutheran's longest-serving pastors. He answered the call to serve the Messiah congregation in 1951 and helped to grow the congregation to more than 200 worshippers on an average Sunday. Petterson retired in 1978. (Courtesy of Messiah Lutheran Church.)

MESSIAH LUTHERAN CHURCH, TODAY. Messiah Lutheran Church continues to do a lot for the community. In addition to being a sponsor of Samaritan House (seen below), the congregation operates a food pantry for the needy and has a clothing bank. The church also hosts a summer vacation Bible school program for community children. (Courtesy of Messiah Lutheran Church.)

SAMARITAN HOUSE. Messiah Lutheran Church was instrumental in the formation of the ecumenical coalition that created Samaritan House, a nonprofit organization that helps to feed and house the poor and homeless in Ashtabula County. The shelter, which opened in 1987, is located in Messiah Lutheran's former parsonage. Since it opened, Samaritan House has served more than 5,300 individuals. (Courtesy of Andrew Holt Frazier.)

BETHANY LUTHERAN CHURCH, ASHTABULA. The Bethany Lutheran Church congregation, founded in 1891 as the New Independent Ashtabula Finnish Evangelical Lutheran Church, was first located on Joseph Avenue and West Ninth Street in the Ashtabula Harbor District. The original church served the growing Finnish community, made up of immigrants who were drawn to jobs on the railroad and later at the Ashtabula docks. (Courtesy of Andrew Holt Frazier.)

BETHANY LUTHERAN CHURCH. Services were originally held in Finnish, but by 1935, as the congregation grew to more than 1,000 members, English services were added, a change that was strongly resisted. The current church, located on Michigan Avenue, was dedicated on October 1, 1955. The large stones on the south wall as one enters the church represent the 26 regions of Finland from which Bethany's founders hailed. (Courtesy of Andrew Holt Frazier.)

St. Joseph's Church, Ashtabula, Ohio

ST. JOSEPH ROMAN CATHOLIC CHURCH, ASHTABULA. St. Joseph Church, located on Lake Avenue in Ashtabula, is one of three churches that make up the Our Lady of Peace Parish. The redbrick church, built in 1905, was renovated in 1969 after the bell tower was struck by lightning. It was again damaged in 2010 in an ice storm and was repaired later that year. The pulpit at St. Joseph Church is made from yellow Siena marble with intricate, marble inlays. Each of the eight stained-glass sanctuary windows is made from approximately 1,000 pieces of glass, framed in lead. Two of the Sacramental Windows, located on each side of the crucifix above the altar, depict peacocks drinking from a cup. Peacocks are an ancient symbol of immortality, and the drinking references worshippers' drinking from the chalice during the Holy Eucharist. (Author's collection.)

FR. JOSEPH SMITH. Fr. Joseph Smith served as the rector of St. Joseph Church from 1894 to 1901. He went on to be appointed a member of the Papal Household under Pope Pius XI and was made vicar-general of the Cleveland Diocese in 1927. He was instrumental in organizing St. Joseph Parish and other Roman Catholic parishes in the area. (Courtesy of Cleveland Public Library.)

ST. JOSEPH CHURCH, TODAY. Our Lady of Peace Parish, including St. Joseph Church, is well-known in the community for its delicious and well-attended Lenten fish fry dinners. The former St. Joseph School is home to Beatitude House, a women's transitional shelter. (Courtesy of Andrew Holt Frazier.)

ASHTABULA HARBOR,
OHIO

Our Mother of Sorrows
Catholic Church

OUR MOTHER OF SORROWS ROMAN CATHOLIC CHURCH, ASHTABULA. Located in the Ashtabula Harbor neighborhood, Our Mother of Sorrows Church is another Ashtabula County church listed in the National Register of Historic Places. The sandstone Romanesque Revival–style church was designed by a German architect and took 300 craftsmen, mostly Hungarian and Portuguese immigrants, two years to complete. The interior measures 100 feet by 60 feet. The church was dedicated in 1900 with 2,000 people in attendance and features life-size statues of the Blessed Virgin, St. John the Evangelist, and Mary Magdalene as well as Carrara marble columns, stained-glass windows, and a three-story belfry. All of the stones used to construct the church weigh at least 200 pounds, and some in the belfry exceed 500 pounds. The exterior sandstone blocks come from Cleveland quarries. In 1907, industrialist Andrew Carnegie donated half of the money needed for a new church organ, with the congregation raising the other half. The organ is still used today. (Courtesy of the Ashtabula County Historical Society.)

OUR MOTHER OF SORROWS CHURCH INTERIOR. The formation of this congregation was also aided by Fr. Joseph Smith (see page 54) and originally met for mass in the Cheney Ship Chandlery Store in the Ashtabula Harbor neighborhood. (Courtesy of the Ashtabula County Historical Society.)

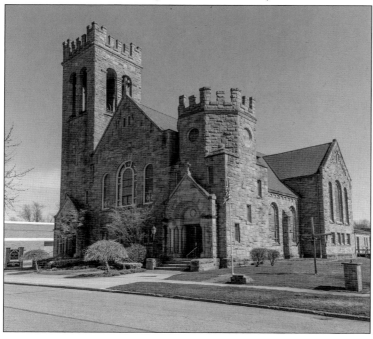

OUR MOTHER OF SORROWS CHURCH, TODAY. Today, Our Mother of Sorrows Church is part of the three-church Our Lady of Peace Parish that also includes St. Joseph Church and Our Lady of Mount Carmel Church. The parish supports a host of Catholic charities, including an annual HALO Christmas food giveaway. Last year, the parish gave away 450 baskets of ingredients for Christmas dinners. (Courtesy of Andrew Holt Frazier.)

OUR LADY OF MOUNT CARMEL CHURCH, ASHTABULA. The third church in the Our Lady of Peace Parish, Our Lady of Mount Carmel Church was founded in 1902 at East Sixteenth Street and Columbus Avenue on the east side of the Ashtabula River. Fr. Joseph Smith also had a hand in forming this parish as well as in seeking the property and in making the real estate purchase with the approval of Bishop Horstmann. It was originally an offshoot of Our Mother of Sorrows Parish in Ashtabula Harbor and was set up to serve the growing Italian population on the east side of the city. The congregation eventually outgrew the original Romanesque and Mission-style church (pictured above), and the current structure at East Twenty-first Street and Columbus Avenue (pictured below) was dedicated in 1974. More than 8,000 worshippers attended the dedication. (Courtesy of the Topky-Harbor Library Archives.)

OUR LADY OF MOUNT CARMEL CHURCH, TODAY. In addition to helping with Our Lady of Peace Parish outreach programs, which include a food pantry, the congregation of Our Lady of Mount Carmel hosts a seasonal produce giveaway in their parking lot on the second Tuesday of the month. (Andrew Holt Frazier.)

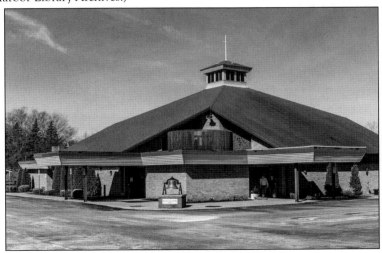

ORIGINAL FIRST PRESBYTERIAN CHURCH STRUCTURE. Rev. Joseph Badger (see pages 13, 14, and 16) was also instrumental in forming First Presbyterian Church in Ashtabula. Badger moved to Ashtabula in 1810 when he ended his missionary work with the Wyandots and, 11 years later, helped to form what would become First Presbyterian Church. The first church (pictured at left), called the Old Meeting House, was dedicated in 1836. (Courtesy of First Presbyterian Church.)

FIRST PRESBYTERIAN CHURCH, 1875. The Old Meeting House, located at the corner of Park Avenue and West Forty-third Street, was moved to the site of the present manse in 1891 and torn down in 1906 to make way for the manse. "Manse" is what Presbyterians call the house, adjacent to the church, where the pastor and his family live. (Courtesy of the Harbor-Topky Library Archives.)

First Presbyterian Church and Manse
Ashtabula, Ohio.

FIRST PRESBYTERIAN CHURCH AND MANSE, ASHTABULA, 1912. Music has always been an important part of worship at First Presbyterian Church. Originally, the church used a melodeon, a small keyboard instrument, but by 1871, they had raised enough for a secondhand pipe organ. That organ was replaced by an $18,000 Steele organ in 1920. The organ was rebuilt in 1970 and is still used today. (Author's collection.)

STAINED-GLASS WINDOWS AT FIRST PRESBYTERIAN CHURCH. The large, intricate, stained-glass windows at First Presbyterian Church illustrate stories from the New Testament, such as the tales of the prodigal son, Jesus at the temple, and the Resurrection. The large Resurrection Window at the rear of the sanctuary is dedicated to Reverend McGiffert, who served the church in the late 19th century and tripled the size of the congregation during his tenure. (Both, author's collection.)

COL. WILLIAM AND KATHERINE HUBBARD. Col. William Hubbard (pictured) and his family were early members of First Presbyterian Church. They moved to the Western Reserve in the spring of 1834. Shortly after arriving, Hubbard joined the Ashtabula County Anti-Slavery Society. His brothers Matthew and Henry, who also lived in the area, were already members. In fact, the duo had founded an abolitionist newspaper, the *Ashtabula Sentinel*. (*History of Ashtabula County*, Williams Brothers, 1878.)

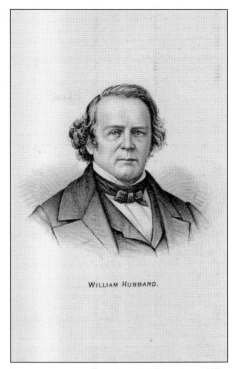

WILLIAM HUBBARD.

HUBBARD HOUSE AND THE UNDERGROUND RAILROAD. The Hubbards' former home is now a museum and is open from Memorial Day to Labor Day. Exhibits include items about the abolitionist movement in Ashtabula County, the Underground Railroad, and the Civil War. There is also an exhibit about the Ashtabula Train Disaster with several artifacts that were recovered from the wreckage. (Courtesy of the Ashtabula County District Library.)

HUBBARD HOUSE. Col. William Hubbard and his wife, Katherine, were some of the first settlers in Ashtabula Village. Their house on Lake Erie on Walnut Boulevard in the Ashtabula Harbor district, built in 1840–1841, was the terminus for four out of five Underground Railroad lines in the county, which escaping slaves used to flee the Antebellum South. Ashtabula County is just 100 miles from the panhandle of West Virginia (then Virginia), and this route was one of the shortest paths to Lake Erie and across to freedom in Canada. For safety, no records were kept about how many former slaves made their way through Ashtabula County. However, one account talks about 39 people being sheltered at Hubbard House during one overnight. Pictured is a door that was used to take slaves from the house to the back lawn and onto Lake Erie. (Courtesy of the Ashtabula County District Library.)

REV. JAMES MILLS GILLETTE,
Pastor 1853 to 1865

FIRST PRESBYTERIAN CHURCH, 1860. The question of slavery was a controversial topic throughout Northeast Ohio in the 1850s and 1860s. The National Presbyterian Church and a new minister, Rev. Jedidah Mills Gillett (pictured at left) at First Presbyterian Church, attempted to stay neutral on the issue. Because of this, 30 percent of the First Presbyterian congregation left the church and formed a new congregation across Park Street in what would become First Congregational Church. Another anti-slavery story involving First Presbyterian Church maintains that church member Jesse McDonald and the previous pastor, Rev. Augustus Pomeroy, spent an entire Saturday night evading slave-catchers and hiding slaves. After finally placing the escaping slaves safely on a boat bound for Canada, they arrived at church Sunday morning in time for the worship service, where Reverend Pomeroy gave the sermon. He claimed no fatigue. (Above, courtesy of the Harbor-Topky Library Archives; left, courtesy of First Presbyterian Church.)

HARRIS MEMORIAL PRESBYTERIAN CHURCH
ASHTABULA, OHIO

DAUGHTER CHURCHES OF FIRST PRESBYTERIAN CHURCH. As Ashtabula's population grew, three other Presbyterian churches grew out of the First Presbyterian Church congregation. As church members moved farther from the center of town, they wanted churches that were closer to their homes. These daughter churches were Prospect Presbyterian Church (now Trinity Presbyterian Church), founded in 1899 on the west side of town; Harris Memorial Presbyterian Church (pictured above), founded in 1911 on the south side; and East Side Presbyterian Church (pictured below), founded in 1918. Harris Memorial Presbyterian Church, named after longtime First Presbyterian Church elder Samuel Harris, has since closed. (Above, courtesy of the Harbor-Topky Library Archives; below, courtesy of the Ashtabula County District Library.)

FIRST PRESBYTERIAN CHURCH. First Presbyterian Church was a pioneer in broadcasting its worship service to the public. While many churches today share their services via social media and other digital outlets, First Presbyterian had its own radio station, WICA, which broadcast the service on alternate Sundays beginning on November 28, 1937. (Author's collection.)

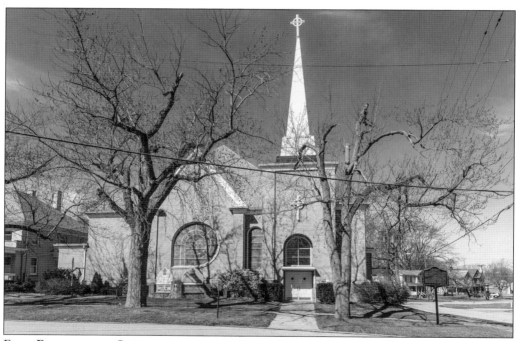

FIRST PRESBYTERIAN CHURCH, ASHTABULA, TODAY. Community outreach programs have always been important to the First Presbyterian Church congregation. The church has sponsored Bloodmobile visits for more than 75 years. They also hosted a vacation Bible school program for more than 100 years, from 1919 until 2020. The church has a blessing box and continues to support area charities, including HALO, Operation Christmas Shelter, and Go Ministries. (Courtesy of Andrew Holt Frazier.)

THE "OLD BUILDING," FIRST UNITED METHODIST CHURCH. First United Methodist Church, located on Elm Street, just down the street from First Presbyterian, was the first congregation to be organized in Ashtabula. The first Methodist "class" (group of home worshippers) was organized in 1812 with six participants, all members of the same extended family. The class was served by a circuit rider who visited groups of worshippers along his 400-mile route. (Courtesy of First United Methodist Church.)

FIRST METHODIST CHURCH, ASHTABULA. The original church building for the First Methodist congregation was a boxlike frame structure constructed on the east side of South Park, around the corner from St. Peter Episcopal Church, on a quarter-acre plot donated by Matthew and Mary Hubbard (see page 93). (Courtesy of First United Methodist Church.)

FIRST UNITED METHODIST CHURCH, ASHTABULA.
The current sandstone church building, dedicated
in 1906, is the Gillmore-Smith Memorial Church,
named in honor of the pastor at the time, Rev.
James Gillmore, and James Smith, who donated
the church land. The sanctuary seats 400 people in
a semicircular pattern, with no seat more than 100
feet from the altar, an important feature in the days
before sound systems. (Courtesy of First United
Methodist Church.)

MARY GILMORE SMITH. Mary Gilmore Smith
(1826–1913) ties together the two families that
played prominent roles in the origin of the present
First United Methodist Church structure. She was
the daughter of the first pastor, Rev. James Gilmore,
and the mother of James Smith, one of the church's
main benefactors. She is buried at Chestnut Grove
Cemetery in Ashtabula. (Courtesy of the Ashtabula
County District Library.)

ASHTABULA TRAIN DISASTER. First Methodist Church was the site of the 1877 memorial service held for the 92 victims of the December 29, 1876, train disaster. During one of the biggest tragedies in Ashtabula history, the Howe truss bridge over the Ashtabula River collapsed as the westbound Lake Shore & Michigan Southern Railway train, the Pacific Express, passed over it, nearing the West Thirty-second Street Station 1,000 feet away from the bridge. All the cars except for the locomotive fell into the gulf, approximately 70 feet below. The rapid descent was bad enough, but the train's oil lanterns and coal furnaces quickly turned the wreck into an inferno. In addition to those killed from the impact, several passengers drowned, and others died from smoke inhalation. Among the dead were hymn composer Philip Bliss and the Reverend Dr. Washborn, rector of Grace Episcopal Church in Cleveland. (Above, courtesy of the Ashtabula County Historical Society; below, *History of Ashtabula County*, Williams Brothers, 1878.)

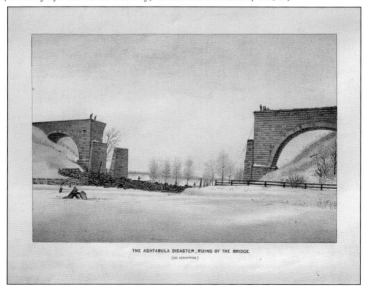

THE ASHTABULA DISASTER, RUINS OF THE BRIDGE.

THE ORIGINAL REREDOS, FIRST UNITED METHODIST CHURCH. A prominent feature in the First United Methodist Church sanctuary is the reredos, the decorative panel behind the altar. This was originally made of dark wood and was replaced with "modern" plastic panels with a "squiggle" pattern in the 1960s. (Courtesy of First United Methodist Church.)

CURRENT REREDOS, FIRST UNITED METHODIST CHURCH. The stained-glass reredos, currently installed in the church, was designed by Pastor Emeritus Rev. Dr. Richard Lehto. The new panels were created by 30 members of the congregation in the church's own stained-glass studio. This installation replaced the Formica "squiggles" and was dedicated in February 2004. (Author's collection.)

STAINED-GLASS STUDIO.
On the second floor of
First United Methodist
Church, there is a
fascinating room filled
with glass pieces, all
sorted and shelved by
color, and a host of
glass-working tools.
The church's reredos
was created here, as was
stained-glass art for the
chapel and other locations
in the church complex.
First United Methodist
Church plans to ramp
up the studio again soon.
(Author's collection.)

FIRST UNITED METHODIST CHURCH, THEN AND NOW. First United Methodist Church offered an ecumenical Sunday school for developmentally disabled children in the 1950s, a time when those children were not given a chance to attend public schools. Current church outreach programs include donating and cooking for local hunger programs, sewing mittens and hats for the needy, and making "comfort bags" for children entering the foster care program. (Courtesy of First United Methodist Church.)

METHODIST EPISCOPAL CHURCH, ANDOVER, 1912. As with other Methodist churches in the county, the church in Andover began its history as a Methodist Episcopal Church, but since the Methodist merger in 1968, it is now a United Methodist Church (UMC). (Author's collection.)

UNITED METHODIST CHURCH, ANDOVER, TODAY. Andover United Methodist Church is active in the community. The church's outreach programs include a free, monthly community dinner; a free Thanksgiving community dinner; a monthly food pantry; and a monthly food distribution in conjunction with the Cleveland Food Bank. The church also has an active youth ministry and a bell choir. (Author's collection.)

First Congregational Church Building Sketch, Andover. The Andover Congregational Church was formed in 1813 when a group of settlers from New Hartford, Connecticut, began meeting at the log home of Zadoc Steele in the western part of Andover Township. As the congregation grew, worshipers met at the Andover schoolhouse, located near the southeast corner of what is now Andover Square. Rev. Giles Cowles (see page 18) and his son Edwin were instrumental in assisting the new congregation. The first church building, depicted at right, was erected in 1843. That church had no pews for the first year and worshippers had to stand during the service. The present church was constructed on the same site in 1908. (Both, courtesy of Andover UCC.)

Congregational Church,
Andover, Ohio.

SUNDAY SCHOOL CLASS, 1940s. Bible study has always been an important aspect of worship at the Congregational Church in Andover. Pictured above is a 1940s adult Bible study class with longtime pastor Reverend Harrison pictured at left. (Courtesy of Andover UCC.)

STAINED-GLASS WINDOWS, ANDOVER UCC. The stained-glass windows at UCC Andover were installed when the present church was built in 1908. They were restored in 1990. The windows depict symbols from the Bible, including the Lamb of God, the Christmas star, the Angel Gabriel, the Easter lily, and the Ark of the Covenant. (Courtesy of Andover UCC.)

ANDOVER UNITED CHURCH OF CHRIST, TODAY. The congregation at Andover UCC continues to make a difference in the greater Andover community. The church's outreach programs include coordinating the annual Back 2 School Bash, an ecumenical initiative to provide 100 percent of school supplies required for needy elementary and preschool-age children in the Pymatuning Valley Local School District, and supporting the Pymatuning Valley Food Pantry. The church's Steeple Stitchers make quilts, blankets, and other hand-sewn items for veterans, those in hospitals and nursing homes, and other groups in need. Church volunteers ring the bell for the annual Salvation Army Kettle Campaigns in July and December. (Courtesy of Andover UCC.)

CHERRY VALLEY METHODIST EPISCOPAL CHURCH, 1920S. The congregation of Cherry Valley Methodist Episcopal Church was organized in 1825 by Elder Davis. Initially, worshippers met in individual homes and were preached to by the circuit riders who visited once a month. The current church building was constructed in 1896 and remodeled in the late 1930s. The church retains many original stained-glass windows, wooden doors, and carved woodwork. (Author's collection.)

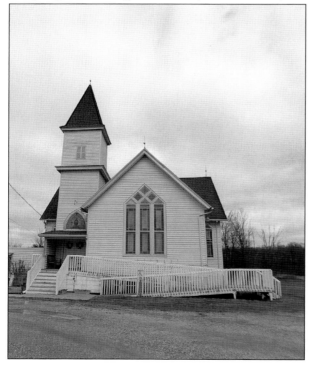

CHERRY VALLEY UNITED METHODIST CHURCH, TODAY. Cherry Valley UMC is a small country church with a distinct personality. Rev. John M. Germaine, the longtime pastor, describes the congregation as "close-knit, but welcoming" and "very dedicated to helping each other and the community." The church hosts a monthly Swiss steak dinner for the public and supports area charities, such as the Andover Food Pantry and the Salvation Army. (Author's collection.)

EXTERIOR OF THE CONGREGATIONAL CHURCH, CONNEAUT. What would become the Congregational Church in Conneaut, now known as Conneaut UCC Church, held its first service in 1803 in Aaron Wright's log cabin with the ever-present Joseph Badger (see pages 13, 14, and 16) leading the service. The church was originally called the Union Church and combined both Congregational and Presbyterian theologies. (Author's collection.)

CONGREGATIONAL CHURCH, CONNEAUT. The first church structure for the Conneaut Congregational Church was completed in 1828. In 1847, the congregation voted to drop their Presbyterian affiliation over the national Presbyterian Church's failure to take a strong stand against slavery. In 1852, the church added a bell. That bell is now in the West Springfield (Ohio) Methodist Church. (Courtesy of the Conneaut Historical Society.)

STAINED-GLASS WINDOWS, CONGREGATIONAL CHURCH, CONNEAUT. The present brick church was completed in 1876 with two figure windows crafted by Tiffany Studios. Other features of the church included bronze front doors, an interior made from Vermont marble, and a cork floor. The church originally had six working fireplaces and sat up to 700 persons. It once had a full gymnasium. (Courtesy of the Conneaut Historical Society.)

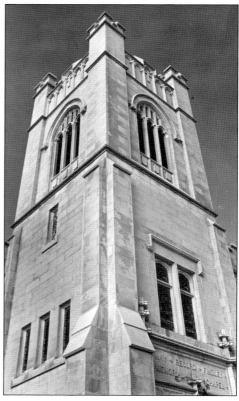

BELFRY, CONGREGATIONAL CHURCH, CONNEAUT. The two figure windows at the Congregational Church depicted the Annunciation and a combination of three women at the cross and the angel at the vacant tomb. The windows were modeled after the windows at Magdalene College Chapel in Oxford, England, and were funded partially by pew fees of between $25 and $500. The pew fees were eventually dropped. (Courtesy of the Conneaut Historical Society.)

First Baptist Church, Conneaut. First Baptist Church in Conneaut was established in 1831 with 26 charter members. The congregation originally met in a schoolhouse at South Ridge and Blood Roads. The first church structure, located on the site of the former Conneaut Post Office, was erected in 1843 and dedicated in 1844. It was made of wood and designed to seat 300 people. The church was heated with a wood stove in the basement and lit by gas lamps. That would prove to be a bad combination. On May 7, 1900, the church's janitor lit the basement stove to heat the church for an evening service and proceeded to go out for supper. Shortly thereafter, two boys saw smoke coming out of the church's front doors. By the time local fire companies responded, the church was ablaze. Poor water pressure made it impossible to successfully fight the fire, and by 10:30 p.m. that night, the church was completely destroyed. Very little was saved. The cast-iron bell fell from the 90-foot-tall spire to the basement and cracked. (Author's collection.)

FIRST BAPTIST CHURCH INTERIOR, CONNEAUT. The current structure (pictured here), located at Mill and Slate Streets, was completed in 1901 and dedicated exactly one year after the fire. The new church was made of brick and had stained-glass windows and natural oak pews and woodwork. It was heated by two hot air furnaces and lit by a chandelier with 16 gas lamps. (Author's collection.)

FIRST BAPTIST CHURCH, CONNEAUT, TODAY. By 1981, when First Baptist Church celebrated its 150th anniversary, church membership had grown from the original 26 members to more than 300 members. (Author's collection.)

FINNISH LUTHERAN EVANGELICAL CHURCH, CONNEAUT. The Finnish Lutheran Evangelical Church was organized in 1895 with 58 Finnish men. The church building, located at the corner of Broad and Erie Streets in Conneaut, was erected in 1901. (Courtesy of the Conneaut Historical Society.)

SUNDAY SCHOOL, FINNISH LUTHERAN CHURCH, 1944. Christian education has always been an integral part of the Finnish Lutheran (now Good Shepherd Lutheran) Church. The church continues to have Sunday school classes between services for everyone ages three and older. (Courtesy of the Conneaut Historical Society.)

Good Shepherd Lutheran Church, 1960s. The Finnish Lutheran Evangelical Church eventually merged with Grace Lutheran Church (see page 124) to become Good Shepherd Lutheran Church. That combined church is now located at the corner of Lake Road and Grove Street in Conneaut. (Courtesy of the Conneaut Historical Society.)

South Ridge Church, Conneaut, 1920s. South Ridge Free Will Baptist Church was first organized in 1826 with eight people. These worshippers met in various homes and businesses until the first church structure was completed in 1837. The congregation changed its name in 1911 from the Free Will Baptist Church to simply South Ridge Baptist. (Courtesy of the Ashtabula County District Library.)

SOUTH RIDGE BAPTIST CHURCH. South Ridge Baptist Church founded South Ridge Academy, a Christian elementary school, in 1973. The church also helped launch WGOJ, a Christian radio station based in Conneaut. (Courtesy of the Conneaut Historical Society.)

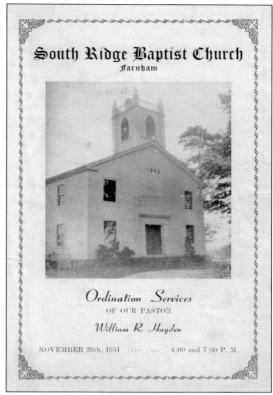

SOUTH RIDGE BAPTIST CHURCH AND THE UNDERGROUND RAILROAD. The pastor's residence, located near the church, was used to house fleeing slaves on their way to Lake Erie and freedom in Canada. The parsonage has a secret chamber in the cellar, and every upstairs room had an opening out onto the roof. The church bell was forged at Buckeye Bell Foundry in Cincinnati, Ohio, in 1860. (Courtesy of the Ashtabula County Historical Society.)

FIRST BAPTIST CHURCH, KINGSVILLE. First Baptist Church, located on the west side of the square in the center of Kingsville, was founded in 1813 with 11 members–four men and seven women. The congregation's first worship services were held in the old Kingsville schoolhouse. The original church building was constructed in 1826 but was lost to fire later the same year. The fire was so intense that the cast-iron church bell melted. The present First Baptist Church building was dedicated in 1910. In 1912, the church bell, recast from the original melted bell, was installed in the new church. First Baptist Church in Kingsville is the "mother church" of First Baptist Church in Ashtabula. (Courtesy of J. Humphrey.)

STAINED-GLASS WINDOWS, FIRST BAPTIST CHURCH. One of the most striking features of the First Baptist Church sanctuary is the church's collection of vibrant stained-glass windows (pictured right and below). There is a large window above the altar and six, smaller windows lining the sides of the church. The windows were taken down, disassembled, re-leaded, and reassembled in the early 2000s. (Both, courtesy of J. Humphrey.)

KINGSVILLE CHURCH. Kingsville Presbyterian Church, the oldest church in Kingsville, was organized in 1810 as a Congregational Church under the leadership of Rev. Joseph Badger. The congregation reorganized in 1844 as a Presbyterian Church. Their first church structure was destroyed by fire in 1848, but they immediately rebuilt at the church's current location on State Route 84. (Courtesy of the Ashtabula County District Library.)

KINGSVILLE PRESBYTERIAN CHURCH. The church was featured in the 1977 television movie *Harvest Home*, starring Bette Davis. The film caused quite a stir in the community since, according to long-term church members, the production team did not originally make clear the satanic theme of the movie. Today, the church is known for its monthly community soup lunches. (Author's collection.)

FIRST BAPTIST CHURCH, JEFFERSON. The First Baptist Church in Jefferson also lays claim to being the first church in the county. The church was organized in 1811 by 18 persons, most of whom lived in Denmark Township. Their first pastor was Elder Judah Richmond, and the first services were held in log cabins and schoolhouses in Jefferson and Denmark. (Courtesy of the Ashtabula County Historical Society.)

First Baptist Church. Jefferson, Ohio

FIRST BAPTIST CHURCH, JEFFERSON, 1930s. The first permanent structure for the First Baptist Church congregation was erected and dedicated in 1836. Membership and baptism by the 19th-century church were only permitted for those who followed the church's strict guidelines. Those who attended dances and otherwise "lived immorally" were not welcome. (Courtesy of the Jefferson Historical Society.)

Baptist Church, Jefferson, Ohio

FIRST BAPTIST CHURCH, JEFFERSON, TODAY. The congregation quickly outgrew this small church, and a new one was dedicated in 1892. The congregation added to the original church by turning it 90 degrees, covering the original wood with brick veneer, and adding electric lights. It was at this time that the church's memorial stained-glass windows were added. This "new" Neo-Gothic church also featured a three-story bell tower and arched sandstone windows and doorways. (Left, courtesy of the Jefferson Historical Society; below, courtesy of Andrew Holt Frazier.)

ST. JOSEPH CALASANCTIUS CHURCH, JEFFERSON, OHIO

ST. JOSEPH CALASANCTIUS CHURCH, 1920S. St Joseph Calasanctius Roman Catholic Church in Jefferson was organized in 1858 as a mission church of the Diocese of Erie, Pennsylvania. The congregation worshiped in various parishioners' homes until 1869, when a church building was constructed. A fire completely destroyed that structure one year later, but it was rebuilt in 1880. The current Spanish-Roman structure was completed in 1925 and features dark tapestry brick and Indiana limestone. (Above, *History of Ashtabula County*, Moina W. Large, 1924; below, courtesy of Andrew Holt Frazier.)

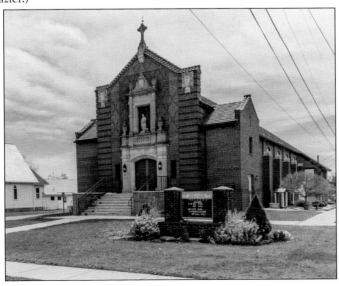

JEFFERSON METHODIST ORIGINAL CHURCH. The Methodist congregation is one of several churches that claim to be the oldest church in Jefferson. The Jefferson Methodists trace their roots back to 1807 when the first Methodist class met in a private home with services led by the occasional itinerant minister. The first Methodist church structure in Jefferson (pictured above) was dedicated on July 22, 1848. (Courtesy of Jefferson United Methodist Church.)

JEFFERSON METHODIST CHURCH AT JEFFERSON DEPOT. The original church building, which has been preserved, is now located in the Jefferson Depot "living history" village. It has a vaulted ceiling and a king-post truss. A horse shed was later added at the rear of the building. The 1848 church was used until the current church was completed and dedicated in 1883. (Courtesy of J. Humphrey.)

JEFFERSON METHODIST CHURCH PARSONAGE. Jefferson Depot moved the original church building to its present location in 1989. Many of the original architectural elements were lost, but the historical society renovated the building using local reclaimed lumber and pews from an abandoned Greene Township, Ohio, church. The church's parsonage (pictured at right), built in 1888 and 1889, was moved to the Jefferson Depot to make room for the new church annex. (Author's collection.)

JEFFERSON UNITED METHODIST CHURCH. The 7,000-square-foot church annex, which features Sunday school classrooms, church offices, a library, a full kitchen and an eating area, a fellowship hall, and a central gymnasium (now a pickleball court), was completed in 1980. The design incorporated the original exterior of the church into the new space. (Courtesy of Jefferson United Methodist Church.)

426D.   Methodist Church, Jefferson. Ohio   Published by Fred Baldwin.

SUSANNA'S CUPBOARD. Susanna's Cupboard, in front of Jefferson United Methodist Church, is named for Susanna Wesley, the mother of Methodism founders John and Charles Wesley. The cupboard is filled daily by church volunteers with nonperishable food items, diapers, toiletries, paper products, and messages of hope and inspiration. Anyone who needs these items is invited to take what they need. Those who are able are invited to leave items. (Author's collection.)

JEFFERSON UNITED METHODIST CHURCH TODAY. Other church outreach programs include the Christian Café, which provides a free community meal twice a month; the health ministry, which provides free health and wellness counseling and referrals to the community; the senior adult ministry, which offers a free weekly lunch, among other activities and services; and work with H2O to provide no-cost home repairs to low-income residents of Ashtabula County. (Courtesy of Andrew Holt Frazier.)

First Congregational Church. Jefferson, Ohio.

FIRST CONGREGATIONAL CHURCH IN JEFFERSON. First Congregational Church, now UCC Jefferson, was organized in 1831 at a time when the entire City of Jefferson was surrounded by forest and had around 300 total residents. Rev. Giles H. Cowles (see page 18) of Austinburg was one of the church's first preachers, along with Rev. Perry Platt and Rev. Ward Childs. The current church building, made from Austinburg brick, was erected in 1835. Funds for the church were solicited from Connecticut and other East Coast donors. The church raised $4,000. One of these donors was Kentucky senator Henry Clay, who gave $10 with the condition that the church not be used to express "sentiments hostile to slavery." (His wish was ignored.) The abolitionist John Brown (of Harpers Ferry infamy) preached here in 1859. (Courtesy of the Ashtabula County Historical Society.)

Photo. by M. A. Loomis, Jefferson, O.

JOSHUA R. GIDDINGS.*

JOSHUA REED GIDDINGS. Joshua Reed Giddings, a prominent Ashtabula County lawyer, and his wife, Sarah, were founding members of First Congregational Church, and he served as a ruling elder (lay leader) of the church. Giddings also represented the county in the US Congress from 1838 to 1855. He was an ardent abolitionist and, with his friend and business partner Benjamin Wade, was largely responsible for Ashtabula County being a hotbed of antislavery sentiment in the years leading up to the Civil War. Joshua Giddings's law office (pictured below), constructed in 1823, has been preserved and is a National Historic Landmark. The office is now owned by the Ashtabula County Historical Society and is open to the public during the summer. (Left, *History of Ashtabula County*, Williams Brothers, 1878; below, author's collection.)

BENJAMIN WADE. Benjamin Wade, Giddings's law partner, and his wife, Caroline, were also members of First Congregational Church in Jefferson. A native of Jefferson, Wade was a self-educated man and an Ohio senator for five years before he was elected to the US Senate in 1851. He served for 14 years and was president pro tempore of the Senate from 1867 to 1869. As such, he was in line to succeed Pres. Andrew Johnson had he been impeached in 1868. If one more senator had voted for impeachment, Wade would have served as president of the United States for the remaining nine months of Johnson's term. Other prominent First Congregational Church members over the years include Quintus F. Atkins, the first sheriff of Ashtabula County, and Elbert L. Lampson, the 21st lieutenant governor of Ohio and a former state senator. Neil Armstrong, who would become the first person to walk on the moon, was baptized at First Congregational Church. (*History of Ashtabula County*, Williams Brothers, 1878.)

FIRST SUFFRAGE CONVENTION. According to a plaque on the side of the Jefferson Congregational Church, the first suffrage convention in the United States was held in Jefferson in 1844. This predates the convention held in Seneca Falls, New York, which is generally accepted as being the first such gathering. According to the plaque, the event was a combination of an antislavery and suffrage event. Betsy Mix Cowles (see page 19) spoke at the event. Researchers at Kent State University (which is home to the Betsy Cowles and Cowles family archives) believe that this event did happen, but it was held two years later than indicated on the church plaque. Cowles also organized and spoke at a suffrage event in Salem, Ohio, in 1850. Cowles was elected president of that convention and, as a result, founded the Female Anti-Slavery Society of Ashtabula County. (Courtesy of Andrew Holt Frazier.)

FIRST CONGREGATIONAL CHURCH, JEFFERSON. The cornerstone for the 1835 church was brought from Windsor via oxen team, a two-day trip. The building also used sand from Ashtabula Harbor and timbers from trees on West Walnut Street. Pew boxes with doors rented for $34 annually, a practice that was eventually dropped. The church was extensively remodeled in 1908, taking on its current appearance. (Courtesy of the Jefferson Historical Society.)

FIRST CONGREGATIONAL, UNITED CHURCH OF CHRIST. First Congregational Church has had several organs throughout its history. The current 628-pipe instrument was installed in 1957. It includes 21 tubular chimes. The church became affiliated with the United Church of Christ when that denomination was created in the merger of the Congregational Church with the Evangelical and Reformed Churches in 1961. (Courtesy of the Ashtabula County Historical Society.)

"Whosoever thou art that enterest this church leave it not without a prayer to God for thyself, for him who ministers and for those who worship here."

The First Congregational Church

JEFFERSON. OHIO.

Rev. J. A. Goodrich, Pastor.

Seek ye first His kingdom and His righteousness.

Strangers and all without a church home are cordially invited to unite with us. Seats are free.

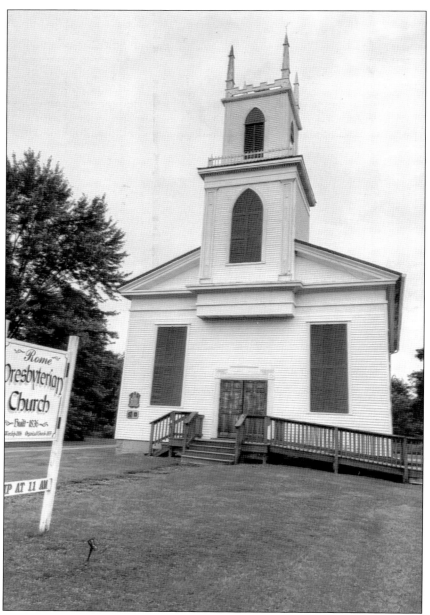

ROME PRESBYTERIAN CHURCH. The congregation in Rome that would become the Presbyterian Church was organized in 1819, another Western Reserve church started by Rev. Joseph Badger (see pages 13, 14, and 16). The church began as a Congregational Church, just like many other Presbyterian churches in the county. The white, Colonial-style structure on US Route 45, near US Route 6, was constructed in 1836 and features flagstones from a quarry in nearby Windsor, Gothic windows, and four minarets that form a crown-like structure above the entranceway. Distinctive green shutters protect the stained-glass windows when the church is not in use. The original, dark wooden pews remain. Rome Presbyterian Church was a station along the Underground Railroad in the pre–Civil War years, and Rev. John Ingersall, a mid-19th-century pastor known for his fervent antislavery sermons, once preached at the church. (Courtesy of J. Humphrey.)

ORWELL PRESBYTERIAN CHURCH. Originally a Congregationalist Church, Orwell Presbyterian Church was organized in 1831 with 15 members from Orwell and nearby Colebrook. In 1837, the members from Colebrook left to form their own church, reducing the Orwell church's numbers to 10. The second sermon at Orwell Presbyterian Church was delivered by Rev. Giles H. Cowles from Austinburg (see page 18). (Courtesy of Grand Valley Public Library Archival Collection.)

THE PRESBYTERIAN CHURCH IN ORWELL. In 1876, the congregation moved and turned the church 90 degrees and built a new addition to the east. A spire was added at the same time, using plans drawn by English architect Sir Christopher Wren. (Although church records state that Wren designed the spire, it must have used an existing Wren design, as Wren died in 1723.) (Courtesy of Grand Valley Public Library Archival Collection.)

LAYING THE CORNERSTONE OF THE ORWELL METHODIST CHURCH, JUNE 1859. The Orwell Methodist Church was organized in 1822 with 12 members. Prior to that, a group of settlers had met in individual homes and even hosted Rev. Giles H. Cowles (see page 18) to give a sermon. The church was part of the Grand River Circuit (for preachers) that included churches in Austinburg, Windsor, and Hartsgrove, among others. (Courtesy of Grand Valley Public Library Archival Collection.)

ORWELL UNITED METHODIST CHURCH. The Methodists in Orwell built a wooden church in 1845 and enlarged and added a bell tower in 1869. The present brick Orwell United Methodist Church was built in 1889. Members of the congregation recall church baptisms being held on the banks of Rock Creek as recently as the 1940s. (Author's collection.)

LENOX FEDERATED CHURCH. The Lenox Federated Church, located at the intersection of Lenox-New Lyme and Footville-Richmond Roads, was built in 1850. It combined members of the local Presbyterian, Congregational, and Church of Christ congregations. In 1922, the church added members of the Methodist and Baptist Churches. This was done primarily for economic reasons, as the small community could not support so many individual churches. (Courtesy of the Jefferson Historical Society.)

LENOX FEDERATED CHURCH, TODAY. The Lenox church has common roots with other churches in the area. Rev. Giles Cowles preached an early sermon to the Congregationalists there in 1813. The small congregation has prevailed and continues to worship together. (Courtesy of J. Humphrey.)

METHODIST EPISCOPAL CHURCH, HARTSGROVE. Hartsgrove Community Church is located in the southwest corner of Ashtabula County, at the southeast corner of US Route 6 and State Route 534. The first religious congregation in Hartsgrove was organized in 1830 as a Methodist Episcopal Church and first met in the home of Calvin Grover until a church structure could be built. There was also briefly an Episcopal parish—St. Paul's Church—in Hartsgrove, organized by the Rev. John Hall from St. Peter Church in Ashtabula, as well as a Free Baptist Church and a Disciple Church. The Methodist church on the square was dedicated in 1867. The current structure, used by Hartsgrove Community Church, was erected in 1894 on the same footprint as the Methodist church. Since Hartsgrove was too small to support all of the denominations in town, they combined to form the Community Church in 1929. (Courtesy of the Ashtabula County District Library.)

M-E CHURCH HARTSGROVE OHIO

HARTSGROVE COMMUNITY CHURCH. A favorite Hartsgrove Church story is about when the floor of the church collapsed. In the 1920s, the church structure was used for community events. During one such event, a 1921 high school graduation ceremony, the weight of the graduating class and the piano was too much for the aging flooring, and the floor gave way, sending everyone in the church to the basement. Fortunately, no one was seriously injured, although one person suffered a broken leg and another a sprained wrist. The women of the church played an important role during the World War II years. The church was unable to continue worship services since all of the men of the church were away, so the Ladies' Auxiliary paid the bills and maintained the church so it would be ready for worship when the men returned at the end of the war. (Courtesy of Grand Valley Public Library Archival Collection.)

ALTAR PAINTING, HARTSGROVE COMMUNITY CHURCH. One of the most dramatic features of the Hartsgrove Community Church is the large mural of the Last Supper located behind the pulpit and communion table. This work, a stylized version of Leonardo da Vinci's 15th-century depiction, was done by Rev. Willard Strong, who served at Hartsgrove Community Church in the 1970s. (Author's collection.)

HARTSGROVE COMMUNITY CHURCH, TODAY. Today, Hartsgrove Community Church is affiliated with the United Church of Christ denomination. The church is well known in the community for its twice-yearly rummage sales, its support of the local food pantry, and its blessing cupboard with food items and blessing bags for needy residents. (Author's collection.)

Two

ASHTABULA COUNTY CHURCHES GONE BUT NOT FORGOTTEN

Despite the best efforts of their congregations, not all churches in Ashtabula County have managed to weather the social and economic changes and shifting demographics of the past 100-plus years. Some churches have succumbed to dwindling numbers and economic challenges. Other churches have combined their congregations with the same or complementary denominations to make more economically viable units. Yet other churches have been reborn as businesses or museums, as detailed in the next chapter.

As lamentable as any church closing is, the legacy of these former churches lives on. Some churches are only a memory, such as the church that used to sit in the middle of the once-thriving Village of Mechanicsville. Some congregations have sold their buildings to those of other denominations. Other congregations have abandoned their expensive-to-maintain church edifices in favor of gathering in private homes or businesses and using the money they save to help the community. The similarity between that scenario and the early beginnings of Western Reserve congregations is striking and ironic.

The stories of these closed churches have much to teach about the people who brought their faith to Ashtabula County and who worshipped there. The memories of services, weddings, funerals, and other activities there remain in the hearts of many Ashtabula County past and present residents.

MECHANICSVILLE METHODIST CHURCH. Mechanicsville was once a thriving community. Located along the Grand River, at the crossroads of what is now Lampson and Windsor-Mechanicsville Roads, the community had a general store/post office, a sawmill and gristmill, the Grand River Institute (see page 22), a tavern, a 10-foot-high dam, and a Methodist church, constructed in 1862. Only the Grand River Tavern and the former parsonage, now a private residence (pictured below), remain today. A huge fire swept through the town in 1889, destroying the church and most of the houses and businesses. A flood two years later wiped out the remaining foundations, the dam, and the ruins of the mill. Hemlock and maple trees have reclaimed the former church site. (Above, courtesy of the Ashtabula County District Library; below, author's collection.)

FIRST CONGREGATIONAL CHURCH, ASHTABULA, 1862. The First Congregational Church in Ashtabula was formed in 1860 when 60 members of the First Presbyterian Church congregation in Ashtabula left that church over the national and local churches' failure to take a strong stand against slavery. This building, located across the street from First Presbyterian Church, was dedicated in 1862. (Courtesy of the Ashtabula County Historical Society.)

FIRST CONGREGATIONAL CHURCH. Originally, the church had a very tall spire, but it was destroyed in the 1870s in a windstorm and replaced with a shorter spire. This spire was removed for safety reasons in 1926, and a flat roof was added. A new organ was installed, and an organist was hired (away from the Presbyterians) in 1878. (Courtesy of the Ashtabula County Historical Society.)

FIRST CONGREGATIONAL CHURCH, ASHTABULA. Electric lights were added to the church in 1901. At the same time, an electric blower was installed to power the organ. Prior to this, a hand-operated bellows was used. Young boys were hired for this job at a rate of $1 per Sunday (for two services). (Courtesy of the Ashtabula County Historical Society.)

CHRISTIAN FAITH ACADEMY. First Congregational Church closed in the early 21st century, and the church was used for several years by the Fellowship Bible Church congregation. Between 2008 and 2022, the space was home to Christian Faith Academy, a kindergarten-through-sixth-grade private Christian day school. The school has since moved to the former Army National Guard Armory on State Street in Ashtabula. (Courtesy of Andrew Holt Frazier.)

ZION LUTHERAN CHURCH, ASHTABULA, 1905. Zion Lutheran Church in Ashtabula was organized in 1890. It was originally called the Finnish Evangelical Lutheran Church of Ashtabula Harbor. The name was later changed to the Finnish National Evangelical Lutheran Church, a name the congregation used until 1949 when it became Zion Evangelical Lutheran Church. (Courtesy of the Ashtabula County District Library.)

ZION LUTHERAN CHURCH. Zion's first church structure was a small frame church, built in 1890. It was used until 1958 when a new structure was built at West Ninth Street and Allen Avenue. The church was noted for its 38-foot illuminated cross in the church's front window. The Zion congregation sold the church building in 2023. (Courtesy of the Ashtabula County District Library.)

St. Paul's Episcopal Church, Conneaut, Ohio.

ST. PAUL'S EPISCOPAL CHURCH, CONNEAUT. St. Paul's Episcopal Church in Conneaut was founded in 1891 by 15 Episcopal women in a local sewing circle who wanted to raise money for land and a church. They raised the needed funds by 1896, and the cornerstone was laid that same year. The English-Gothic–style church was designed by the Cleveland architectural firm of Thayer and Wilson. It was made entirely of stone with stained-glass windows, a slate roof, and a stone belfry. The exterior walls are between 12 and 14 inches thick. The four-ton cast-iron bell and the white oak altar were donated by the Diocese of Ohio bishop at the time, the Right Reverend William Leonard, and his wife. In 1993, the altar and reredos from St. Michael's Church (closed) in Unionville were installed at St. Paul's. The church was well-known in the 1950s for its fish dinners. St Paul's closed in 2002. The space is currently being used by Lighthouse Free Will Baptist Church and the Brotherhood of Gods Disciples Jefferson Chapter, a motorcycle ministry. (Courtesy of the Ashtabula County Historical Society.)

St. Mary of the Immaculate Roman Catholic Church, Conneaut. Located on Chestnut Street, this early Conneaut church began in 1850 as a mission church of the Painesville parish of the same name with once-a-month worship services. Mass was first celebrated in individual homes. It was not until 1864 that the first frame church building was constructed. (Author's collection.)

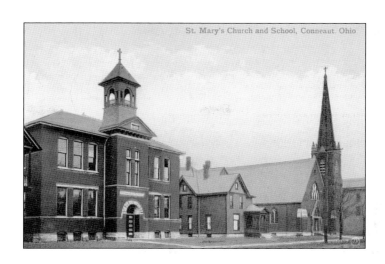

St. Mary's Church and School, Conneaut. Ohio

Wedding at St. Mary of the Immaculate Church, 1940s. The last church building for this parish, located on State Street in downtown Conneaut, was completed in 1887 and dedicated in 1888. It is made from brick and stone and of an English Gothic design. St. Mary's closed in 2023. The congregation of this parish was combined with that of St. Frances Cabrini Parish. (Courtesy of the Conneaut Historical Society.)

1904

HOWARD, PHOTOGRAPHER, ORWELL.

THE DISCIPLE CHURCH.

DISCIPLE CHURCH, ORWELL. The Disciples of Christ of Orwell was organized in 1853 with 30 members. The church stopped holding services after a few years due to dwindling numbers but reorganized in 1889. The congregation lacked the funds to hire a full-time pastor, so they were served by student preachers from Hiram College, a liberal arts college affiliated with the Disciples of Christ. (Courtesy of Grand Valley Public Library Archival Collection.)

PRESBYTERIAN-DISCIPLE CHURCH   ORWELL, OHIO.

A NEW DISCIPLE CHURCH. The congregation sold the church building to the Orwell School Board in 1910 and constructed a new church in East Orwell. The original church was used by the Roman Catholic congregation for a period and later by a Mennonite congregation. It was divided into apartments in the 1960s. (Courtesy of Grand Valley Public Library Archival Collection.)

Three

ASHTABULA COUNTY CHURCHES WITH A NEW PURPOSE

Ashtabula County boasts a large number of creative business owners and civic leaders, who have looked at abandoned church buildings in the county and seen the potential for innovative retail spaces, theaters, and museums. The county is somewhat unique in this regard. Most of these spaces retain some of the architectural elements of their church past and are recognizable as former places of worship.

Not only are these businesses and museums that have been created out of former church spaces unique, but saving these historic buildings from being razed is laudable and ecologically responsible. It is also economically sound. In many cases, it would be prohibitively expensive to recreate elements like stained-glass windows and hand-carved wooden moldings, even if it were possible. Some raw materials like chestnut wood are simply not available today.

The former Ashtabula County church spaces lend an elegant and serious air to the stores, wineries, museums, and theaters that now occupy them. Owners, managers, and organization leadership are to be lauded for seeing the potential of these churches and saving them. Hopefully, others will follow their lead.

First Congregational Church, Geneva. The former Congregational Church (later the Geneva Masonic Lodge; see page 26) gained a new purpose when it was purchased in October 2022 by Noble Arts Entertainment, a theater company that has been hosting dinner theater productions in Geneva-on-the-Lake since 2008. (*History of Ashtabula County*, Williams Brothers, 1878.)

Noble Arts Entertainment. The theater company has kept many original architectural elements, including some of the stained-glass windows, the tin ceiling, and the oak woodwork. The former sanctuary of the church will be the main theater and seat around 300 people. The narthex will be the theater's lobby, and the former cloakroom will be transformed into the ticket booth. The new theater space is expected to open in summer 2025. (Author's collection.)

CONGREGATION OF THE FIRST HUNGARIAN REFORMED CHURCH IN CONNEAUT, 1960. The congregation of the First Hungarian Reformed Church in Conneaut was created in 1899 with a group of 33 Hungarian immigrants from Fairport Harbor. Led by Zsigmond Barra, the church was officially chartered in 1910. The First Hungarian Reformed Church structure, built in 1914, is made of red brick with a square bell tower. (Courtesy of the Conneaut Historical Society.)

NORTH COAST D-DAY MUSEUM, CONNEAUT. The North Coast D-Day Museum is an extension of the annual D-Day reenactment that happens each August in Conneaut Township Park. The museum, which opened in 2016, is located in the former First Hungarian Reformed Church. It features an eclectic collection of World War II memorabilia and artifacts, including uniforms, weapons, and gear. The free museum is open from Memorial Day through Labor Day. (Author's collection.)

TRINITY EPISCOPAL CHURCH IN JEFFERSON. Trinity Episcopal Church was founded in 1837 with four members from Austinburg, Ashtabula, and Jefferson. Services were held in a schoolhouse until a church building was constructed in 1846. The cornerstone for the present American Gothic–style church was laid in 1876. The 19th-century author William Dean Howells was baptized in this church. (Courtesy of the Jefferson Historical Society.)

TRINITY EPISCOPAL CHURCH INTERIOR. The small church once housed a huge M.P. Moller organ, built in 1873. The organ has since been sold, but the building still has its original stained-glass windows, hardwood floors, and carved wooden pews. The wooden baptismal font also remains. (Courtesy of the Jefferson Historical Society.)

TRINITY EPISCOPAL CHURCH. Henderson Memorial Library, located next door to the former Trinity Episcopal Church, purchased the church building in 2000 with plans to use the structure for lectures and other library events. Later, Jefferson Play-School remodeled and rented out the back portion of the church, the former fellowship hall. (Courtesy of the Jefferson Historical Society.)

JEFFERSON HISTORICAL SOCIETY. The fledgling Jefferson Historical Society bought the building in 2005 and restored it to its 1923 appearance. Today, the former Trinity Episcopal Church houses a variety of artifacts and information on the history and development of central Ashtabula County. The back room is used for the society's library. The lawn is used for the seasonal Jefferson Farmers Market, held each Saturday from May through September. (Courtesy of J. Humphrey.)

CHRIST EPISCOPAL CHURCH, WINDSOR MILLS, OHIO. Christ Episcopal Church in Windsor Mills, in the southwest corner of Ashtabula County, was one of the first churches to be established in the county. Founded in 1816 by the first Episcopal bishop of Ohio, the Right Reverend Philander Chase, the church was, very briefly, the mother church of the Episcopal Diocese of Ohio. It was here that the first Episcopal Convention in the Western Reserve was held. The original church edifice was built by Solomon Griswold and dubbed "Solomon's Temple." It served parishioners until a more permanent structure was built on the same footprint. The Christ Episcopal Church structure currently in Windsor Mills was built in 1832 to resemble the Greek Revival–style churches of Connecticut. The 32-by-40-foot church features a curved supporting beam ceiling, hand-carved solid walnut pews, a balcony, and a unique raised pulpit. (Courtesy of Christ Church Geneva.)

CHRIST CHURCH. Christ Church began to languish almost as soon as the new structure was built. In 1891, the Diocese of Ohio listed "Grace Church, Windsor" as being extinct (that is, no longer an Episcopal church). However, the error in the name allowed the church to survive, and it continued to be used periodically for weddings and funerals for several more decades. (Courtesy of Grand Valley Public Library Archival Collection.)

CHRIST CHURCH INTERIOR. It is no coincidence that the elements of the current structure look like a New England house of worship, as the earliest European settlers in Ashtabula County hailed from Connecticut. In fact, the shutters on the church were taken from the Connecticut governor's mansion in Hartford. (Courtesy of Ashtabula County Historical Society.)

CHRIST CHURCH, WINDSOR MILLS, 1950. The Methodists used Christ Church for a time in the early 20th century until they built their own chapel nearby in 1932. The well-built church edifice remained structurally sound even though it had fallen into disuse by the 1950s. The building attracted the attention of the Ashtabula Historical Society, and it was leased to the society in 1955. Using original plans for the church, the society carefully restored the building and opened a museum in the space. (Both, courtesy of the Ashtabula County Historical Society.)

CHRIST CHURCH INTERIOR, WINDSOR MILLS. A variety of unique materials were used in the restoration. The back doors come from the old Jefferson post office. The front doors once graced the entrance to the Leonard C. Hanna mansion on Cleveland's Euclid Avenue (also known as Millionaire's Row), and much of the lumber was taken from the dismantled grandstands at the Ashtabula County Fairgrounds. Some of the flooring is from the old railroad station in Williamsfield. After the 20-year lease expired, the building was leased by the Windsor Historical Society, which operates the museum today. The building was placed in the National Register of Historic Places in 1975. (Above, courtesy of the Ashtabula County Historical Society; below, author's collection.)

FORMALITY BRIDAL. Geneva Baptist Church, on US Route 20 across from University Hospital Geneva Medical Center, has found new life as a bridal gown emporium. Formality Bridal, under the guidance of owner Penny Bowers-Schebal and her staff, matches brides with affordable yet beautiful gowns. The church's stained-glass windows, Gothic arch, and a few pews remain, giving the space a reverent, elegant air. (Author's collection.)

INSIDE FORMALITY BRIDAL. The former pastor's office is now the bride's dressing room, and the original Bible closet is now used to store sewing supplies and odds and ends. The remaining pews were refinished and are now used on the "stage," where the bride's family views her in her new gown. Bowers-Schebal particularly likes that the space has the feel of an "old country church." (Author's collection.)

WINDOWS INSIDE FORMALITY BRIDAL. The original stained-glass windows give Formality Bridal a regal and elegant ambiance. The collection of 16 windows illustrates stories from the Bible, such as this one that depicts the story of Noah's ark. The windows line both sides of the showroom. There is also one in the bride's dressing room. (Author's collection.)

FINNISH LUTHERAN/GRACE LUTHERAN CHURCH. The congregation that would become Grace Lutheran Church was organized in 1901 with 26 members. The small brick church building was constructed in 1902 but not dedicated until 1916, due to the lack of a pastor. The bell tower was added in 1926, and chandeliers and stained-glass windows were added in 1949. (Courtesy of the Conneaut Historical Society collection.)

HEAVENLY CREAMERY. Heavenly Creamery opened in 2019 in the former Grace Lutheran Church. The popular Conneaut ice cream shop is open seasonally and offers 130 flavors of homemade ice cream. The repurposed church retains the building's original stained-glass windows and much of the hand-carved woodwork. (Author's collection.)

SOUTH RIVER VINEYARD. South River Vineyard in Harpersfield Township is located in a former Methodist Episcopal Church that dates back to 1892. The vineyard's tasting room is located in the former sanctuary, which still features the original woodwork, flooring, wainscoting, hand-carved pews, and leaded-glass windows. Vineyard owner Gene Sigel found the abandoned church in Shalersville, Ohio, near Kent, and moved the structure to his Ashtabula County vineyard piece by piece. The vineyard, one of 32 wineries in Ashtabula County, opened in 2002 and specializes in growing vinifera grape varietals and producing Lake Erie pinot noir, Riesling, and ice wine. (Both, author's collection.)

BIBLIOGRAPHY

75 Years of Grace: 1915–1990. Geneva, OH: St John's Lutheran Church, 1990.

Butler, Margaret Manor. *A Pictorial History of the Western Reserve 1796–1860.* Cleveland, OH: World Publishing Co., 1963.

Campbell, Edward C. *Geneva, Ohio: The Building of an American City: 1866–1966.* Geneva, OH: Lions Club of Geneva, Ohio, 1966.

Feather, Carl E. and Ruth Feather. *Ashtabula County, Ohio: A Field Guide.* Geneva, OH: The Feather Cottage Media, 2018.

Feather, Carl E. *Ashtabula Harbor, Ohio: A History of The World's Greatest Iron Ore Receiving Port.* Geneva, OH: The Feather Cottage Media, 2017.

——. *Hidden History of Ashtabula County.* Charleston, SC: The History Press, 2015.

Galbeath, Charles B. "History of Ohio." The American Historical Society Inc., 1925.

Geary, Linda L. *Balanced in the Wind: a Biography of Betsey Mix Cowles.* Lewisburg, PA: Bucknell University Press, 1989.

Hatcher, Harlan. *The Western Reserve, The Story of New Connecticut in Ohio.* Indianapolis, IN: the Bobbs-Merrill Company, Inc., 1949.

Knepper, George W. *Ohio and its People.* Kent, OH: Kent State University Press, 1989.

Large, Moina W. *History of Ashtabula County.* Topeka-Indianapolis: Historical Publishing Company, 1924.

McGiffert Rev. J. *History of The Presbyterian Church in Ashtabula, Ohio.* Ashtabula, OH: James Reed and Son, Printers and Publishers, 1876.

Rice, Harvey. *Sketches of Western Reserve Life.* Philadelphia, PA: Williams Brothers, 1885.

——. *Historical Sketch.* Austinburg, OH: Grand River Institute, 1924.

——. *Our Parish.* Geneva, OH: Assumption Church, 1965.

Robertson, Stacey M. *Betsy Mix Cowles, Champion of Equality.* Boulder, CO: Westview Press, 2014.

Rolofson, Robert H. *Through Succeeding Years: A History of the First Presbyterian Church, Ashtabula, Ohio.* Privately printed, 1939.

Wickham, Gertrude V. *Memorial to the Pioneer Women of the Western Reserve.* Cleveland, OH: Centennial Commission, 1896.

Williams, William W. *History of Ashtabula County.* Philadelphia, PA: Williams Brothers, 1878.

INDEX

DISCOVER THOUSANDS OF LOCAL HISTORY BOOKS FEATURING MILLIONS OF VINTAGE IMAGES

Arcadia Publishing, the leading local history publisher in the United States, is committed to making history accessible and meaningful through publishing books that celebrate and preserve the heritage of America's people and places.

Find more books like this at
www.arcadiapublishing.com

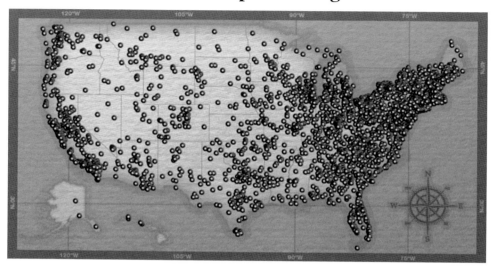

Search for your hometown history, your old stomping grounds, and even your favorite sports team.

Consistent with our mission to preserve history on a local level, this book was printed in South Carolina on American-made paper and manufactured entirely in the United States. Products carrying the accredited Forest Stewardship Council (FSC) label are printed on 100 percent FSC-certified paper.

MADE IN THE
USA